AF255448

Little Big Moments

Little Big Moments

51 Playful and Piercing Lessons
about Parenting

Andrew Taylor-Troutman

RESOURCE *Publications* · Eugene, Oregon

LITTLE BIG MOMENTS
51 Playful and Piercing Lessons about Parenting

Resource Publications
An Imprint of Wipf and Stock Publishers
199 W. 8th Ave., Suite 3
Eugene, OR 97401

www.wipfandstock.com

PAPERBACK ISBN: 978-1-6667-6766-7
HARDCOVER ISBN: 978-1-6667-6767-4
EBOOK ISBN: 978-1-6667-6768-1

05/26/23

All Scripture quotations are taken from the New Revised Standard Version Bible, copyright 1989 National Council of the Church of Christ in the United States of America.

In memory of Jerry Jerome Hanley, who taught me that baseball and young children are precious and holy and deserving of all the attention we can give them. Granddad also made the best cookie salads ever.

I think if you have your ears open, if you have your eyes
open, every once in a while some word . . . will flame
out—and these are the moments that speak our names in
a way we cannot help hearing.

—FREDERICK BUECHNER

Contents

Section 2: Little Big Moments
When You Are Not Alone

Author's Note

He wrote the way a child skips rope, the way
a mouse dances. —E.B. WHITE

MANY READERS MAY KNOW E.B. White as an accomplished writer of such children's classics as *Charlotte's Web* and *Stuart Little*. Mr. White was also an editor, and several of his fellow inky ilk have helped this book to play and dance, notably Kathy Hanrahan, Bill Horner, Paul Isom, and April Williams. Many of these chapters first appeared in the *Chatham News + Record* and WRAL's *Go Ask Dad* blog. I'm grateful to each of these editors for working their magic and even more for the magic of their friendship.

I'm most grateful to my wife, Ginny, without whom no magic is possible for me.

I'd also like to thank the three kids she and I love best: My dear ones, I have tried to write with the unpretentious, carefree joy that Mr. White's images call to mind. I hope that, one day, each of you will find a measure of whimsy and humor in these pages. This probably won't happen when you are teenagers, but who knows? Wonders never cease—just look at the three of you.

Andrew Taylor-Troutman

Chapel Hill, North Carolina

Section 1: **Little Big Moments When You Know You Are Enough**

Ode to Hoodies

As an undergrad, I occasionally pulled a hooded sweatshirt over my bedhead for the trudge across campus to my early morning classes. But I became a hoodie devotee in the caffeine-fueled years of graduate school. There was a table in the back of the student center with items free for the taking, mostly used textbooks and chipped coffee mugs. Occasionally, I would find gently used clothes. Beggars can't be choosers. I snatched hoodies bearing the politically incorrect logos of professional sports teams.

Over the past fifteen years of marriage, Ginny has personally overseen my wardrobe upgrade. But left to my own devices, I'm likely to walk out of our house dressed like a rumpled twenty-something. (I tell myself that the coffee stain on the sleeve is not *that* noticeable.) Except for one upgrade: now that I am employed, I purchase my preferred style hoodie with the zipper in front.

I marked our family's return to North Carolina with a UNC hoodie, Ginny's alma mater. Yet, I still have a hoodie from a university near where we used to live in Virginia. I've held onto it because I wore it on the day we came home from the hospital with our firstborn. I'm still amazed that bona fide healthcare professionals would let a clueless guy like me leave with a newborn. At least I wasn't wearing cargo shorts at the time.

Last week, I pulled this hoodie out of the back of the closet and could almost smell the sour milk. Maybe that whiff wasn't just my imagination. Our first baby would spit up as regularly as the Old Faithful geyser. I'd clean up the best I could, then cradle him against that sweatshirt as he napped, pulling the hood low over my eyes to rest myself.

He is now ten years old. Kids grow up and clothes wear out, though a father like me tries to hold onto both.

I still keep a (relatively) clean hoodie on the coat rack by our back door. Our dog gets all jumpy whenever she sees me reach for it, knowing it's time for a W-A-L-K. After I have leashed her, I'll often invite my eldest to come along. He has his own life now: graphic novels, video games, friends down the street. Most often, he turns down his dad; I respect that he needs his own space.

But sometimes he'll accept my invitation. Grinning, I'll hand him a certain article of clothing. We'll both zip up and off we go.

The Best Dad Gift

It's not another coffee mug. Get out of here with your shirts and ties. No right-minded person would even consider giving me a power tool. Cologne? Are you serious?

Whether the gift is for Christmas, Father's Day, or my birthday, I always prefer to receive socks. Yes, socks—the wildest, wackiest, coolest socks.

I actually have socks that read "Here Comes Cool Dad." I've been given other socks with pictures of goats and acoustic guitars. A yeti-like creature playing a guitar. Snowpeople playing guitar (a theme, yes). Socks with baseballs and footballs and fútbols. I received socks with a picture of my dog's face emblazoned on them.

And the pièce de résistance—socks with a picture of a cat wearing sunglasses while flying through space . . . on a slice of pepperoni pizza!

Someday, it would be awesome if one of my kids knit socks for me. Or maybe created some with a 3D printer. Who knows? In the meantime, they search the internet with their mom.

I have socks with peace signs and Mister Rogers quotations. Smiley-face emojis and pink hearts. And tacos, which I like to sport on Tuesdays.

As a pastor, I own several pairs of nondescript black socks that I wear to most funerals, although recently I wore the peace sign socks in honor of one woman, and her widower loved it.

On Sundays, however, I wear the funky socks—"funky" in terms of the artwork, not the smell. Still, people have noticed.

Maybe a few make comments behind my back, but it's a welcoming church. Express yourself!

A young boy approached during a recent Sunday service and, grinning widely, hitched up the leg of his khakis to reveal socks with Chewbacca! I happened to be wearing my space-cat socks, which I gleefully showed him. Obviously, he was impressed.

This is a boy who, like many kids his age, will wear gym shorts, even if the wind chill is a smaller number than his age. But his mother convinced him to wear "church pants" by promising that he could wear his Chewbacca socks. And that I would be wearing funky socks, too!

She didn't necessarily think that he would show off those socks during the worship service, but I certainly didn't mind. In fact, his grin was the best present of that day. Quite possibly the holiest moment. We worship a "God who laughs and plays" according to the medieval mystic Meister Eckhart.

My kids know not to get me baseball caps or golf balls. No gardening or grilling tools. Gift cards are fine. But would I rather have a pair of wild and wacky socks? Does a cat fly through space on a slice of pizza?

Home

Home. Try saying it out loud, slowly. If you are reading this in public and worried that onlookers will look at you funny, you could whisper very quietly.

Think of the two sounds you make when you say it: ho-muh. Do you feel how your lips come together and apart like a kiss at the end? Ho-*mwah*!

I have written this book from my home. My home "office" is really just a desk in the bedroom I share with my wife, Ginny. It is my work space where I pay the bills, answer emails, and write what I call playful and piercing lessons about parenting.

When I sat down to write this morning, a toy monster truck waited on top of my laptop, a little surprise from my five-year-old daughter.

On the same desk, I keep a picture of this daughter posing with her two big brothers a couple of years ago. They stand in a row from oldest to youngest. All three are on scooters, each sporting a big smile beneath their helmets. This photo was taken by Ginny on the sidewalk in front of our home, the very spot I see through the second-floor window before my desk.

Beside this picture of our kids is a card from my beloved that reads, "My Heart Has Found Its Home with You." I often read this card out loud. A kiss to myself.

When Ginny and I decided to have children, we thought about where we wanted to make our home and how we would afford to live there. We discussed logistics like jobs, healthcare, budgets, housing markets, and taxes. (Actually, her father is a certified public accountant. We left the taxes to him.)

One thing we did not discuss was infertility. In my experience, that is something you only talk about when you can no longer avoid it.

In the beginning, I rallied quickly from each monthly disappointment. Maybe that's a guy thing or maybe because I was a former athlete—get 'em next time! Ginny felt she was being punished like Prometheus; each month, her heart grew back only to be devoured out of her chest again.

As our infertility struggles continued, I worried that my marriage would end. Ginny never led me to believe that. In fact, she assured me of just the opposite.

But my worst fear was that I would not be enough.

That fear manifested itself as voices of insecurity and shame, which lived rent-free in my head. Even now, I still find that I have to evict them. A dear friend taught me a yoga mantra: You are enough. You have enough. You do enough. You are enough.

You are enough.

I hold this mantra right beside My Heart Has Found Its Home with You.

The building that is my home is three stories high and less than 1,800 square feet—"tall and skinny like you," Ginny smiles. In a few moments, I'll get up from my desk and amble down the narrow hallway in my cat-flying-through-space-on-a-slice-of-pizza socks. I'll note the permanent marker scrawled on the wall in cryptic circles next to the paint that has been chipped away from flung toys. In the living room, there will be Legos and Pokémon cards strewn across the floor like paint on a Jackson Pollock canvas. Stuffed animals congregated in nearly every place save for the bins where they are supposed to be stored. The table festooned with capless markers and broken crayons and scraps of paper from dismembered coloring books. And there is always a random sock lying on some piece of furniture.

I will also see my family. It is enough. It is home.

Prayer

My wife and I are both pastors. Ginny and I try to teach our kids about holy things. We learn about holy things from our kids. The other night before bed, the middle child whispered to his mom, "I think I have God and Mother Nature in my heart." I mean, c'mon! What a dear!

But it is likewise true that all three of our children raise holy hell when it is time to say grace before meals.

Picture the five of us around the table, our food before us. Either Ginny or I will begin to offer simple words of gratitude; it's not like she and I pontificate in long-winded supplications. But almost immediately, all three of them start to complain. Sometimes they even yell, "Stop!"

I think God is rather amused by this behavior—the Lord created all preacher's kids!

I also understand that their responses to prayer represent a power struggle. My kids do not decide whether or not to go to church on Sunday mornings. So, they push back when they can. Such differentiation from one's caregivers is a healthy part of growing up. I certainly am not the only parent that faces this reality.

A 2022 Gallup Poll found that in American houses of worship, attendance has dipped below 50 percent of the population. For the first time in eight decades, a majority of our citizens do not belong to either a mosque, synagogue, or church. Does this cause Christians to doubt their words and actions, even their own faith?

These are not abstract questions for me. I am a pastor, part of the church as an institution.

I am also a parent and a person of faith. When my kids' antics annoy me, even anger me, it's important to step back and ask myself, "What's going on *with me*? Why is their behavior triggering me? Is it that I wish to have pious children?"

Naw, that can't be it. Something deeper is going on.

My kids trigger me at the dinner table because I doubt my parenting abilities. Am I able to pass along to my offspring the shimmer of the faith, that which has helped me in my darkest hours? Am I able to teach them to pray, to trust, to hope?

The Gallup Poll brought to mind my maternal grandfather. Granddad was what some call a "lapsed Catholic," meaning he no longer darkened the church doors of his youth. When I was a boy visiting for a weekend, I liked that he and I could stay home and watch Sunday morning cartoons. Okay, I *loved* that about my visits. Instead of church, he and I would play baseball in the yard, pretending we were teammates on his beloved Atlanta Braves. We would head inside when it got too hot and sit at the kitchen table for a cookie salad—a couple of Oreos, a couple of Chips Ahoy, tossed together in a bowl.

But though I never remember Granddad going to church, grace was always said before meals. Granddad offered a prayer from his Roman Catholic upbringing that sounded like one long word:

BlessusOLordandtheseThygiftswhichweareaboutto-
receivefromThybountythroughChristourLord.

I am going to keep praying every night before meals. Saying grace is about the recognition that the life-sustaining gifts of food before us did not magically appear on our doorstep through Amazon delivery, but required work at every step from farm to factory to grocery store to kitchen to table. Whether named as God, Allah, Jesus, a Higher Power, the Source, or the Universe, we are all indebted to forces beyond our ken.

That kind of preachy talk would make my kids roll their eyes.

Though he had left the church, Granddad held onto the prayer of his childhood. Something about his faith stayed with him and must have been a part of the kind, patient, generous, and loving way that he related to me. Now that is my prayer for my kids.

Ray

Ginny traveled to the mountains for a week with friends—a much needed break for her and an opportunity for me to spend more time with our three kids.

I picked up our youngest from preschool at noon. After lunch, our puppy whined at the back door. Our daughter said she'd wait in the kitchen while I took the dog outside.

Stepping back into the house a few minutes later, I saw a stool pushed over to the pantry. We keep the cookies on the top shelf.

I commented on the stool's location. My daughter stared at me. I asked if she had been eating cookies. She vehemently denied this. When I asked again about the stool, she claimed that our neighbor had moved it and then raced out the front door!

The dog found the bowl of half-eaten cookies on the couch before I did.

My daughter has been lying more and more often. There have been little lies like not washing her hands or brushing her teeth. She also stole a classmate's stuffed animal and fabricated this elaborate tale about how her teacher had made it for her. The same toy with a "Made in China" tag!

After dropping her off at preschool the next morning, I shared this story with two fellow parents over breakfast. They were sympathetic. My friends are also pastors, so we fell into a conversation about sin. Occupational hazard. We were ordained in different denominations, but there's a standard belief among Protestants that "all have sinned and fallen short of the glory of

God" (Romans 3:23). Even little kids. The doctrine of original sin maintains that we are born that way.

But other Christian thinkers have believed that, instead of original sin, there is original blessing—we are all created good. There's a biblical warrant for this idea too: "I am fearfully and wonderfully made" (Psalm 139:14). Pelagius, a fourth-century monk, claimed that a "ray of divine light exists at the heart of every person."

That "ray of light" is something for modern preachers and parents to consider.

Dr. Becky Kennedy, clinical psychologist and host of the popular parenting podcast *Good Inside*, seems to believe in a form of original blessing. She insists that when children lie, they "aren't trying to manipulate their parents to avoid getting in trouble." Rather, we have evolved to notice what keeps caregivers close and what pushes them away. Dr. Becky's key idea: "Our kids lie to preserve their connection to us."

"As an adult, you aren't to blame for your child lying," Dr. Becky assures listeners of her podcast. Yet, she also challenges us: "You are responsible for thinking about what is going on and you are responsible for taking the lead to create an environment where there can be more trust, so your child feels safe to share the truth."

To shine their light.

The following afternoon, my daughter and I were crayoning pictures at the kitchen table. I had to take a phone call. I could hear her move upstairs to her room. She slammed her door. I finished the call and went to investigate. I knocked first. There was frantic rustling, then the door opened.

After a sweeping glance into the room, I needed to take a deep breath. Then, I reminded my daughter that paints are not allowed upstairs because accidents happen on the carpet. Like right there!

"My brothers did it!"

I asked about the fresh paint streaked on both of her arms. Her lower lip began to tremble.

I took another deep breath and invited her to sit in my lap on the floor. We sat in silence for a few moments as rays of light streamed through her bedroom window. I told her that I knew it was hard without Mommy here. I missed her, too. I told my daughter that I would always love her. There was nothing she could do that would make me love her any less.

"Not even if I draw my picture on my brothers' wall?"

"Not even that."

"So . . . can I do it again?"

Yes

"Dad, all you ever say is 'no'!"

Obviously, that is an exaggeration. I use other words. For example, when my six-year-old begged for his own cell phone, I replied, "Absolutely not!"

It's true that Ginny and I forbid certain things for our three children as well as limit other treats like desserts and video games. Our children are not cows given free range (neither are they grass-fed). Most parenting experts, as well as parents themselves, would agree that it is the caregiver's job to set boundaries for the child's safety and well-being. Your kid might protest, maybe scream and slam doors, even threaten to throw your own cell phone into the toilet. But you stand firm.

Recently, our oldest asked if he could camp in the backyard with his siblings. Ginny and I looked at each other, wordlessly considering the costs—minimum safety risk but likely a late bedtime, leading to grumpy kids that next day. She grinned and I knew the answer:

"Yes, you can."

And also, we said yes to pizza for supper. Yes, your friend down the street can join us. Yes, we will build a fire. Yes, you can feed sticks into the flame. No, you cannot try to leap over the fire like in a video game. S'mores? YES!

Our eldest son eats only chocolate and graham crackers. Our youngest stuffs marshmallows in her mouth like a blonde chipmunk with pigtails. Only the middle son takes the time to build the classic s'more. His mom taught him how to hold the marshmallow on the end of his stick at just the right distance from the flame and turn it ever so slowly, toasting it to a golden brown.

When the moon was high and bright, the neighborhood friend went home. The fire was settling down and my kids were still amped on excitement.

Clinical psychologist Dr. Becky Kennedy says on her *Good Inside* podcast that "two things are true"—a parent can set the boundary (it is bedtime) and also be empathic, thereby validating the feelings of the child (you want to stay awake). Certain things are nonnegotiable, and I also try to remain open to my children's perspective. They often turn to wonder and end up teaching me.

No, you may not go wake up the dog. No, you may not go look for owls. No, you may not get out of the tent at all!

Yes, we can look at the constellations.

As we stayed inside the tent, staring up at the night sky through the mosquito netting, the youngest began to count the twinkling stars. She got up to twenty, then skipped to "Fifty-seventy!" Yes, we all laughed.

It is a caregiver's job to set boundaries. And also to give thanks for abundance, for "most this amazing day" as E.E. Cummings put it, and "everything which is natural, which is infinite, which is yes."

Flarp

WHAT IS "FLARP"? SEE if you can guess the correct definition of the word based on ten factual events in my recent past.

1. Flarp is having to cancel the last vacation of the summer, on the morning of, due to the father of the household testing positive for COVID-19.

2. Instead of unpacking the roughly 300 items necessary to take three young children anywhere for 24 hours or more, a flarp is dumping the full suitcases in various places all over the house.

3. According to most medical opinions, including guidance from the CDC, people infected with COVID-19 can expect at least 90 days of virus-free protection. Flarp is when the virus fails to read the fine print of said guarantee.

4. Flarp refers to the specific kind of groan that an otherwise healthy, fully vaccinated and boosted 41-year-old dad makes when lying in bed unable to sleep due to dull body aches from COVID-19.

5. Actually, a flarp is the sound made by a reusable grocery bag stuffed with a fully prepared supper when carried up the steps to a sick person's front door.

6. When best friends invite non-isolating children and spouse to their home for a scavenger hunt with clues to guide them from the front door to an inflatable swimming pool, then to

the backyard playground, whereby Ring Pops are discovered to have been taped to the swings, a flarp is the noise of a joyous four-year-old popping said Ring Pop from her mouth with gusto.

7. At the end of this scavenger hunt at the aforementioned home of dear friends, when the last clue leads to a gift-wrapped box that contains all manner of sweets and goodies, a flarp refers to the harmonized squeal of the four-year-old with the shouts of exultation from older siblings, six and nine years old, respectively.

8. Upon receiving texted images of beloved children during scavenger hunt, a flarp is the sigh of wonder from the father infected with COVID-19—flarp in equal parts awe and gratitude to the aforementioned best friends and to his loyal spouse, who surely has the verve of a saint!

9. Flarp is "noise putty" that was found in the gift-wrapped box at the end of the scavenger hunt. It looks like regular putty, but when compressed into its plastic container, the putty makes a noise that the COVID-19-infected father's Gran would hope he would refer to in print as "passing gas."

    (In truth, his Gran would not like for him to refer to "passing gas" in any sentence that likewise contains her name, but he's pretty sure she wouldn't mind just this once.)

10. A flarp is a writer's effort to wield humor, patience, and creativity at a difficult, disappointing situation in his life in hopes to bring a smile or perhaps a chuckle to his readers and possibly inspire their own grace under duress, which if said writer was pressed to boil it down, is as true as anything he knows. We are in control of so very little save how we react and who we love.

Dad Jokes

My two-year-old nephew was playing with a rubber ducky in his water table on my parents' back porch. I asked him what the duck said and, before he could answer, I woofed like a dog. He smiled. Then, I meowed like a cat. He started to giggle. My own father, who was watching nearby, mooed like a cow! My nephew collapsed onto the deck with laughter.

Later that evening, as I related this story to my slightly older children, my nine-year-old rolled his eyes: "It's not as funny as you think, Dad."

Sometimes my jokes are plain silly. But most people think of Dad Jokes as bad puns. A Dad Joke results in a smile with a shaking head or a groaning laugh.

Why is the letter "A" like a flower?

Because a "B" comes after it!

What is the scariest tree?

Bam-BOO!

Not exactly the height of comedic art. My kids also say these jokes are "corny." This expression was originally used by jazz musicians to refer to old-fashioned tunes or styles of playing that might be heard in rural areas like at a barn dance. It's true that a Dad Joke is not like a tuxedoed stage performer or incisive political commentator. But if you don't take yourself too seriously, you can laugh at your own expense.

What do you call a flight service for older dads?

Receding Airlines!

Why did the rooster go to the gym?

To work on his pecks!

Maybe your father told you that laughter is the best medicine. Science has proven that a hearty guffaw or even a short chuckle releases endorphins—hormones that relieve stress and produce pleasure. My young nephew got a full-body workout from rolling around the porch. My own spirit was lifted as well.

Laughter is also spiritual nourishment. I understand the problems with imagining the deity as our Father in heaven. God is spirit, not made in our own image. And plenty of people suffer from abusive fathers, which can hinder if not prevent them from worshiping Love Divine.

But maybe it wouldn't be such a bad thing to think of the Higher Power as uttering the occasional Dad Joke. I mean, just look at the platypus!

I suspect that dads are behind the puns on many church signs like, "God answers knee-mail" and "Soul-er powered by Son-shine." The congregation that I serve decided not to install a sign with removable letters, which is probably a good thing for all who happen to pass by. I try to limit my Dad Jokes to the dinner table, not the pulpit, but I might be tempted by a marquee. And you, gentle reader, might wish I had exercised more discretion with this essay, which originally appeared in my local newspaper.

Speaking of which, I asked my son for a newspaper the other day.

"Don't be so old-fashioned and corny, Dad. Use the iPad."

That fly never knew what hit him!

Cherry

Famous children's book author Margaret Wise Brown once remarked wryly to a former professor, "When you talk to a child, he may not be listening to you at all. He will just be feeling the fur collar of your coat."

Yes, the author of *Goodnight Moon* and other children's classics featuring cute little animals did wear an awful lot of fur.

More importantly, her simple observation also conveyed Brown's guiding mantra known as "here and now." She believed that children focus upon objects that appeal to their senses in the moment. This laser-like fixation can be maddening when you are late for an appointment, and you've already told your child to put on his shoes three, no, *four* times! But noticing the here and now can also be holy.

Melissa A. Butler is a teacher, writer, and consultant whose work revolves around "the art of noticing" what is before us. According to Butler's website, this noticing approach "honors the wisdom and immensity of small things." I have learned this paradox of the immensity of small things from my children who, like many kids, are resident experts of the here and now.

The other day, in my parents' basement, my son and daughter played for 30 minutes with a single red balloon. They began by batting it in the air, trying to keep it from hitting the ground, and shrieking with laughter when it did.

Tiring of this game, my daughter suggested that they name their balloon. After a brief yet intense caucus, they agreed upon

Cherry. My son declared that Cherry was freezing, which meant that it needed to be nestled in a bed of old blankets. A few minutes later, Cherry was ready to get up, and they all tromped to the other side of the basement where they were promptly ambushed by imaginary monsters! My kids defended Cherry with karate chops and flying kicks; the balloon suffered no collateral damage in the melee.

In her book, *How to Notice*, Butler advises adults to make time to "wonder" (in both senses of the word) about small objects with their imaginations: "Let yourself play, notice what happens." Through noticing with patient, holy attention, we can make sense of the huge, often overwhelming world. We can wrap our minds around what we can wrap our arms around.

As poet William Blake put it, "Hold Infinity in the palm of your hand."

Before my children dashed upstairs for lunch, they handed over Cherry to my safekeeping. As I held the balloon, I remembered when my kids were not much bigger and how I cradled them when they were red-faced from crying.

"There, there," I'd soothe them. "You are safe. You are loved."

This memory was a small thing. But the wonder of it was that I realized how badly I need to hear those same assurances: *You are safe. You are loved.* I suddenly felt lighter. Cradling Cherry, I headed upstairs to be with my loved ones.

Parenting Lessons from My Puppy

Our kids had begged for a puppy, pledging to do their part to care for our newest family member. Their hearts were in the right place. I've had dogs before, so I was not naïve about the amount of time and energy involved in training them . . . or about who would actually do that work.

But what I've learned this time around is how dog training lessons give insights into parenthood. It turns out you can teach old parents new tricks.

Lesson 1: You don't have to shake hands.

We name our puppy Ramona after Beverly Cleary's character, our favorite literary hero. Our Ramona likewise has a mind of her own.

She is always willing to sit because she knows that she will be rewarded with a treat. She has trained me very well.

But even the promise of a doggie biscuit will cause her to lift her left paw only about a third of the time. This was frustrating to me until my four-year-old daughter clarified, "Daddy, Ramona doesn't have to shake if she doesn't want to."

Children are often asked to give hugs and kisses on command. I feel it is important to communicate love and appreciation for others, yet it's not fair to expect kids to be touched against their will. They should be in charge of their own bodies.

I'm particularly sensitive to this need for bodily autonomy for girls, and my daughter named it!

This leads me to another life lesson . . .

Lesson 2: If you want something, speak up!

Ramona's piercing bark drives me up the freaking wall; I've been known to yell back at her! Let me tell you how completely ineffective this reaction is.

By contrast, when she starts barking, my son gets quiet and still. More often than not, he settles her down by getting her breakfast or letting her outside to pee or sitting down to snuggle with her on the couch.

"Dad," he quietly says, "I can speak dog."

There's no question that he figures out what Ramona needs by listening. Not yelling.

Many others have noted the irony that parents spend the first years of their children's lives coaxing them to walk and talk, then the following years barking at them to sit still and be quiet. In truth, my kids can whine with a grating intensity that exceeds any canine I've ever met. Again, I'm up the freaking walls!

But just as I know it's not helpful to yell in response, I believe it's crucial for them to communicate their needs, including from a young age.

When I was growing up, my mom would tell me that it was holy to know what you want. Granted, the world does not revolve around you and your parents are not genies in a bottle! But that doesn't mean you shouldn't share your feelings and desires. We have different desires and needs, which reminds me of the next lesson . . .

Lesson 3: You need your own space.

I correct my children when they refer to Ramona's crate as her "cage." We are not locking her up. Her crate is not a form of punishment, but rather her own space where she can rest.

She also cannot chew the new chair from her crate!

But the larger point is that Ramona needs her own place in order to feel safe. She's not the only one.

My nine-year-old recently crawled into the empty crate and pulled the door behind him. "Dad," he grinned, "the crate is great!"

He's a poet and an introvert!

Between his two young siblings and our rambunctious dog, there's a lot of energy pulsating through our house. After supper, our oldest often retreats to his room. I love spending time with our entire family together. Yet, I'm learning to give him space when he needs to recharge in his crate, I mean, his bed.

Lesson 4: It's the journey,
not the destination.

The kids and I took our pup on a walk through the woods. Ramona tugged on the leash, desperate to show those gray, bushy-tailed acrobats a thing or two. While the kids left the trail to investigate mushrooms, ferns, and rocks, I grew impatient for us to get going . . . until I realized that we really didn't have anywhere to go. This walk wasn't about getting our steps or reaching some distant milestone. I could relax, enjoy the moment, free from expectations, and . . .

Hey look—a squirrel!

Give a Dad a Rodent

WE GOT A DOG about a year ago. But instead of sating their desire for pets, my children wanted another animal. It is easy for me to get out of buying my youngest a unicorn. (Like many things, I can fault the supply chain.) The middle one makes noise about bringing home an otter, but videos of these creatures dancing seem to scratch that itch.

But the one persistent, ongoing request from all three kids is for a hamster.

It was my idea to name our dog Ramona after Beverly Cleary's beloved character, so I might have anticipated that my kids would be drawn to a hamster after reading *The World According to Humphrey* series by Betty Birney. Birney's Humphrey is a beloved classroom hamster who gets into all sorts of fun adventures.

But he's still a rodent.

I complained about my plight to a colleague and friend who promptly launched into a speech regarding the superiority of guinea pigs to hamsters. I couldn't tell the finer points of his argument. He lost me at rodent.

It's not that I never make compromises with my brood. Just this morning, my five-year-old demanded to go to school in only her underwear. I carted her off to school in a Wonder Woman Halloween costume—a compromise with sparkly sequins!

Perhaps you are thinking I should give a hamster a try. Well, I had a gerbil as a kid. I remember the stinky cage. It's not that I don't trust my kids, but I've picked up their shoes too many times to believe that they can consistently handle disposing of hamster poo. You might argue that my children could rise to the challenge of this newfound responsibility, but the idea of a pet is different from the reality of being responsible for one. To paraphrase the ancient Greeks, 'tis sweet to look at hamsters through the window of a pet store.

My kids are persistent. They know that, compared to their mother, I'm the one more likely to cave. To stay strong, I repeat the dictum of ancient Chinese philosopher Lao Tzu: give a dad a fish and he will eat for a day; give his children a rodent and he will spend weekends cleaning messes and searching for lost rodents under his couch.

Gold Star

Lying next to my six-year-old son in the bottom bunk one night, I listened as he reviewed that day's art class, specifically how he had learned to draw stars. He had two main techniques: first, draw a diamond, then a triangle on top of it.

I interjected that this design was known as the Star of David. You know, after the guy in the Bible.

"Dad," he sighed, "don't bring the Bible into it."

The poor preacher's kid!

He then explained his second star-drawing method: a square with four tiny triangles attached to the corresponding four sides.

I kept my mouth shut. But I thought about how my middle child was breaking down a shape to its simplest parts. This reminded me of a friend who had introduced me to Stuart Shanker's book *Self-Reg*. The title refers to "self-regulation," which is actually different from self-control. Rather than inhibiting impulses, self-regulation is about "identifying the causes and reducing the intensity of impulses."

The book's premise is that there is no such thing as a "bad kid." Janet Lansbury, another parenting expert, believes in the exact same idea. I heartily reply, amen! Instead of viewing a child's actions and attitudes as misbehaviors, and therefore evoking a punitive response, we should study the young person's "behavioral cues" in order to identify the basic aspects of the environment that could be upsetting the child and triggering disruptive behavior. If that sounds simple, then you've got the idea.

In promoting self-regulation in the classroom, Shanker asks caregivers and educators to consider specific changes to the environment. It can be as simple as closing the door to cut down on the noise in the hallway or dimming the overhead lights. Small yet significant changes can lead to the adjustment of the most important environmental factor—the adult-child relationship.

Earlier that day, my son threw himself on the floor and screamed until his face was red. He was upset that dinner wasn't ready. I tried to reason with him—it was only 5:00! When that didn't work, I started to raise my voice in frustration.

My wife, however, left supper cooking on the stove, then turned off the news radio. Ginny cut the overhead light and flipped on the lamp by our sofa. She fluffed one of the pillows and invited our son to sit and rest. As she spoke to our son, her tone of voice was mellow and melodic, her gestures slow and rhythmic.

After a moment, a noticeable calm settled over him.

She then explained that dinner would be ready soon. He got up and happily started to draw.

I'd give both Ginny and our son a gold star—a square with four tiny triangles. They took a complex emotion and broke it down into its simplest parts, which allowed them to process the big feelings and eventually move on.

Later that same evening, my son yawned next to me in his bunk bed. "You know, Dad, you can also make stars in the sky just by making dots."

It's true that, sometimes, the simplest things are best. I might add that "wisdom comes from the mouth of babes," but I could be accused of bringing the Bible into it!

Yogis

You can observe a lot by just watching. —Yogi Berra

"Our society values hot takes and tweets more than sustained thought," claims Scott Hershovitz. In his book, *Nasty, Brutish, and Short: Adventures in Philosophy with My Kids*, he suggests a different understanding of the ancient command "to change and become like little children" (Matthew 18:1). This teaching is often interpreted as adults having the faith or trust of a child, perhaps a similar innocence or playfulness.

But Hershovitz believes children are natural philosophers: "Little kids (age 3-8) often raise philosophical questions on their own. They're puzzled by the world—and they're trying to puzzle it out."

As I drove my three young children to school one day, my nine-year-old piped up from the back of the minivan: "Sometimes telling the truth is not a good idea."

"Tell me more," I replied, channeling how Hershovitz responds to his children.

"If someone is wearing a stupid hat and he asks you what you think about it, it's better not to hurt his feelings."

"But you shouldn't lie," interjected his six-year-old brother. "That would be bad."

"Why is lying bad?" I prompted.

"You could hurt someone's feelings," he answered.

"So, in your brother's example, you could hurt someone's feelings with the truth, but you could also hurt someone by lying. What should you do?"

This philosophy lesson in the carpool wasn't scripted or planned in advance. Kids think about the world around them all the time. Adults can listen and ask follow-up questions rather than impose ready-made answers. You don't have to teach in law school, like Hershovitz, to encourage your children to make an argument.

My nine-year-old switched tactics: "I don't see how George Washington ever became president."

"How come?" I asked.

"My teacher said that he never told a lie."

"So, you're saying you have to lie to become president? Why is that?"

"Dad, sometimes people don't want to hear the truth," he explained.

"But you should still tell it!" the six-year-old maintained.

This was a good argument regarding the absolute truth versus the relative nature of truth. Both boys puzzled over larger ideas through the lenses of what they'd been taught and their own experience. Rather than simply swallow one perspective, they modeled the importance of wrestling with the view from the other side.

A common drive to school can turn into a fascinating inquiry into truth because children are willing to wonder and be open to other views. Hershovitz claims that philosophy is not about winning or losing an argument. Rather, quoting Bertrand Russell, philosophy has "the power of asking questions, which increase the interest of the world and show the strangeness and wonder lying just below the surface even in the commonest things of daily life."

As we pulled into the school parking lot, my nine-year-old wrapped up our conversation by concluding, "It's more complicated than you think when you actually think about it."

Maybe he is more like the great philosopher Yogi Berra.

Okay Being Me

Across the street from my home is an alley where it is more or less safe for children to ride bikes and scooters. What a phrase, "more or less"—how can it be both? A paradox, like terror and delight, which more or less describes my mental state as I watched two of my children divebomb down the steep hill on their wheels, leading the gang of neighborhood kids.

The youngest rode her scooter, balancing one leg in the air behind her like a mini-ballerina, and the middle (not to be outdone) stood on the pedals of his bike. Both whooshed past, hollering, "Watch me, Daddy!"

Oh, I watched! Watched with the certain knowledge that I'd be helpless to keep either one from harm in the event of a fall. I could envision blood, broken bones, and grisly combinations thereof.

And it also delighted me deep in my own bones to see their obvious pride in their skills and the comradery with other kids.

Meanwhile, my eldest quietly circled me in wide loops on his scooter. All by himself. When the younger two children had safely stopped at the bottom of the hill, I considered him. Why was he alone? Should I tell him to join the others?

Clinical psychologist Becky Kennedy, a.k.a. Dr. Becky of the *Good Inside* podcast, believes that adults should stop using "shy" as a negative label for children. We tell teenagers, "Don't do something just because the other students are doing it." But we turn around and say to children, "Go and play with the other kids!" Why do we affirm teenagers for standing up to the crowd, while insisting that younger kids join their peers? That's not a paradox, but an inconsistency.

Many of us are well-intentioned. If children pull away from their peers, we worry about their social skills and their self-confidence. Because shyness often carries the burden of negative connotations, psychologist Barbara G. Markway coined the term "slow to warm up." But I wonder if that, too, is not stigmatizing.

Dr. Becky points out that you can confidently say, "No, thank you." Confidence is not defined by participating in a sport or performing on stage. Confidence is the ability to let others know what you need and claiming, "I'm okay being me."

It is not unusual that my younger son would be a part of the neighborhood pack engaged in a common activity. As the pandemic restrictions eased, he wanted to do every organized activity: T-ball, Cub Scouts, tae kwon do . . . and that's just in one week! He loves the social aspects of being with other children as much as the activities themselves.

Likewise, it fits that my older son would hang by himself. He wants little to do with extracurriculars. He has two good friends to play with in the neighborhood, yet he will also happily retreat upstairs to his room with a book. He's been this way his entire life. As a little boy, he could amuse himself for hours with Matchbox cars. On road trips, he used to stare out the window, lost in his thoughts. He has a rich inner life. My wife and I did insist that he join Cub Scouts. He enjoys it, but he is also adamant: "Dad, that's enough for me."

No two people are exactly alike. As a parent, for me the key is trusting each of my children to know themselves. It may be appropriate to nudge my older son into a new activity, just as it might be necessary to rein in my younger son from too many. But there shouldn't be negative judgments about wanting different things and for being different. My oldest son can gain self-confidence in other ways besides sports or group activities. I need to trust him to take the lead. When my older son was only two-and-a-half years old, he told a kindly yet insistent older woman, "I need my space." He had the self-confidence to know what he needed.

As his brother and sister trucked their way back up the hill, I watched my oldest son stop riding his scooter and look up at the blue sky. I looked at the sky, too. To have one's head in the clouds or to stare off into space can be a wonderful thing.

Mustache: A Must Have?

MUSTACHES ARE BACK! I see mustachioed men at the grocery store, the gym, and the coffeeshop. I'm not the only one who has noticed. Manscaped, a men's fashion company, recently claimed in a blog post, "Mustaches [are] all over the place, and everyone seems ok with it."

My wife would beg to disagree.

When Ginny and I were in seminary, certain students didn't shave for the entire month of January in order to participate in Sketchy Mustache Night. That January 31, she took one look at me and shrieked in horror!

While some might think that "sketchy mustache" is redundant, the look of 1970's Burt Reynolds or Tom Selleck is back in vogue. The Mustachaissance is likely assisted by television stars Nick Offerman and Milo Ventimiglia as well as Miles Teller of *Top Gun* fame. Around town, I've seen versions of Teddy Roosevelt's shaggy walrus 'stache as well as an honest-to-God handlebar.

Should I, too, sport a bristle baton, a flavor savor, a mouth mirken?!

Dramatically changing my appearance didn't cross my mind when my children were young. But now they are old enough not to freak out. Heck, most of the time they ignore me anyway.

Maybe I'll hold off until "Movember"—Mustache November that brings awareness to men's physical and emotional health, including prostate cancer and suicide prevention.

But my wife still bashes the 'stache, so it's doubtful that I'll don a lip sweater anytime soon.

I admit that my 'stache-interest might well reflect a midlife crisis. I'm forty-two years old. AARP is more likely to email me than Manscaped.

Could I be mo' like the young hipster dads?

At least as crises go, mine is very minor. There are plenty of dads with outrageous tattoos.

Combat Gender Roles

MY SONS HAVE STARTED a neighborhood gang. The Combat Club. The boy down the street is the other member. They practice their tae kwon do moves on each other and flex their little biceps. Darling.

The rival gang that roams the same street does not have an alliterative nickname yet boasts 33.3 percent more members. All of them are female. These girls play house in my neighbor's garage, while the boys punch and kick the air.

I wonder, what happened to everyone playing in the backyard? The sandbox and clubhouse are still there. They used to find all kinds of things to do together.

But now the oldest kids are in the fourth grade.

Maggie Dent, a prolific parenting author, noted that many school systems treat boys differently from girls by upper elementary school. For example, a girl may aggressively shove a boy and receive no punishment, while a boy accidently bowls over a girl and gets detention.

Dent believes such differentiation begins even younger. If a young girl falls over, adults might say, "Aw, sweetheart, are you hurt?" But a boy would be told, "Brush it off, you're alright." I can see how these double standards would lead to an all-male Combat Club.

Instead, Dent would have adults say the same thing to all children: "I see you fell down. Do you need a grown-up's help?" This communicates to the child that they are capable and also that an adult is available. It also signals to the other children that everyone is being treated fairly. Dent's observations, which stem from decades of research, cause me to think that the supposed rivalry between the boys and girls in my neighborhood may well stem from competing expectations given by adults.

The members of the Combat Club tromped into the backyard the other day. I asked if they were having fun; they struck a few muscle poses for my appreciation. Then, four girls zipped down the alley on their scooters. Innocently, I inquired of the boys if they, too, wanted to ride.

"We want to fight!"

I shrugged. It was their choice. They hustled off to fight bad guys or something like that.

But not ten minutes later, I happened to see a gaggle of kids on scooters—"gaggle" being the technical term for three boys and four girls. After they had ridden up and down the block a few times, everyone came barging into the backyard. "Dad! We're all hungry!"

At least these kids have equal expectations of a certain adult.

The ABCs of Monotasking

I HAVE AN APP on my phone that opens my email, so I can answer messages while waiting in line for after-school pickup or eating a quick lunch by myself. But the other night Ginny was explaining something to me about our kids before dinner . . . and I don't know the details because I was also firing off an email!

Multitasking is not good (either for my marriage or for my mental health). Yet, I tend to pride myself on making good use of otherwise nonproductive times.

How "productive" is this multitasking?

Earlier this summer, Matthew Sloan, executive editor of *Harvard Men's Health Watch*, published an article on "the art of monotasking." Research proves that trying to do multiple things at once results in more mistakes and less retention of information. Instead, your focused attention on one task is far better for higher functioning activities like work (or listening to your spouse). Monotasking makes intuitive sense to me.

Why do I still act as though multitasking is a good use of my time?

Much of multitasking is a result of the anxiety that I am not doing enough. There are important tasks to do at church. There are many problems in the larger community, such as affordable housing, access to healthcare, water pollution, climate change, racial inequity, gun violence, substance abuse, poverty . . . the list goes on and on! There's no time to lose—I must tackle multiple things at once!

Frederick Buechner was a minister and writer who invited readers to find "the place where your deep gladness meets the world's deep need." In daily life, this is both an invitation and a challenge.

Writing in tribute to Buechner, David Brooks confessed in *The New York Times*: "Perhaps like many others, I struggle to experience my inner life in the quiet, patient, deep and old-fashioned way that Buechner experienced his. So much of the world covers over all that—constant media consumption, shallow communication, speed and productivity." In other words, the glorification of multitasking.

Far better, then, to look for your deep gladness and the world's deep need by paying attention right where you are. In addition to older mentors and astute writers, my children teach this lesson to me—even though one of them can barely read.

I worked on my phone one afternoon while my four-year-old daughter colored next to me. I was trying to answer emails; she demanded my attention. She wanted to write a back-to-school letter to her friend, which detailed her summer vacation. Her written vocabulary basically includes her name, so she needed my help. I had to dictate each word, letter by letter: P-O-O-L and B-E-A-C-H. Her list went on and I grew restless, my fingers itching for my phone.

Then, it dawned on me: what was the most important thing I could do at this exact moment? It was not to send an email for someone to read later.

I spelled the words for my daughter, but she was the one teaching me a sacred lesson.

Good Struggle

Before I had kids of my own, I thought "helicopter parenting" was an extreme sport. Let's also try bungee-jumping parenting and skydiving parenting!

The truth is quite serious. In this case, "helicoptering" refers to a hovering caregiver, an adult anxiously watching for the opportunity to swoop in and rescue the child. For example, adults who keep their hands just inches from the young one climbing a slide on the playground.

Of course, no one wants their kid to get hurt. But there's also the danger that our best intentions can inadvertently harm our children. Helicoptering may prevent children and adolescents from learning to do things for themselves long after their playground days.

My friend has adult children and is a professor at NC State University. Because one of his sons attends that university, he is a member of two NC State parent Facebook groups. There are lots of helpful discussions in the groups, such as "what kind of computer does my child need?"

But threads can also cross into helicopter territory.

In those cases, the parents assume responsibilities that could have been learning opportunities for their children. In the most alarming posts, parents decide what classes or instructors their children should take. They have their children's cars fixed. One parent was even looking for a cleaning service for a student apartment.

I admit that I, too, am guilty of helicoptering. It is natural to want to help one's own flesh and blood! But before swooping in, I find it helpful to ask, who am I really trying to help? Is my child in real and present danger? Or, is the actual problem that I am uncomfortable watching them struggle?

Author Janet Lansbury encourages caregivers to practice such self-awareness. Instead of helicoptering, Lansbury describes "elevating child care" as allowing children "to face age-appropriate struggles." In her work, Lansbury builds on the theories of Magda Gerber, a pioneer of parenting advice in the twentieth century, but the idea of elevating child care goes back even further.

Long ago, Paul of Tarsus wrote that "suffering produces perseverance" (Romans 5:3). The original Greek for "suffering" referred to pressing down on something (or someone), while the word "perseverance" literally meant to remain under a weight. It is not always helpful to helicopter in and pull out a loved one from a difficult situation, for "perseverance produces character" (Romans 5:4). "Character" originally described a coin made out of refined metal. Metal is refined or purified by pressure and heat.

I am certainly not suggesting that anyone put their kids through the ringer! No one wants children to suffer.

But a *struggle* can be good for them. Instead of zooming to the rescue, sometimes adults can help by backing off so that they can lift themselves.

Parenting is an extreme sport—it can be extremely difficult to watch your child fail, even at something fairly innocuous. But, whether the challenge was for a four-year-old daughter to climb to the top of a slide or a twenty-four-year-old son to return to college, my friend and I have never been prouder of our children than when they have climbed to a pinnacle on their own. Instead of helicoptering, we have used our hands to applaud.

Turtle Shells

Santa gave my sons *Super Mario Kart 8* this year. I was just as excited about playing this race simulator. Not to brag, but I was the champion of my fraternity house. As we got the game set up on our TV, part of me wondered if I should take it easy on my kids. After all, it was Christmas.

Nintendo is new to our home, but Ginny and I have had many conversations about competing against our children. Do we play the wrong card and putt past the hole? Or, do our best and help them learn how to lose?

Child psychologist Lyn Fry recommends the latter. "If a child always wins," she claims, "they'll never learn how to cope with adversity."

But what about instilling self-confidence from basking in the glow of victory? Fry anticipates that question: "Children will feel no pride if they know they've won a rigged game." Of course, part of being a parent means I have to cope with the adversity of their meltdowns when they lose. To avoid this discomfort, I have sometimes stacked the deck in their favor. I have let the air hockey puck slide into my goal.

Would I lay off the accelerator in *Super Mario Kart*?

My older son was happy to let me pick my character first. I chose Luigi because he was tall and skinny like me. "He's also slow like you," my son added.

That's when I decided that, temper tantrum or not, he was going to eat my dust! I was the former Kart champion! Just who did this little punk think he was?

After the first lap, I had to admit he had gotten pretty good from playing at a friend's house down the street. He raced as Toad, a mushroom-capped dude who was the smallest yet quickest driver. I'd outmaneuver him on the curves, putting that college experience to good use, but he'd make up ground on the straightaways.

We were neck-and-neck until the start of the third lap when he miscalculated a gnarly curve and fell into the abyss. While he had to wait for his car to be put back on the track, I cruised ahead to the glory of the finish line . . .

BAM! A flying turtle shell hit Luigi from behind and I spun off the track. My son raced past and won. Attacking your opponents with turtle shells is totally legal in *Super Mario Kart*. His victory was fair and square.

Back in the fraternity house, I would have chucked my controller with curse words. But being a parent means being the adult in the room.

"Good race," I said through gritted teeth. After he finally stopped his wild victory dance, my son shook my hand with a surprisingly firm grip, and I thought about how time is faster than any cartoon racer. Before I know it, he'll be wasting tuition money playing video games and learning priceless life lessons along the way.

But I didn't have time to wax philosophically. His younger brother was waiting for the next race. Since I lost, I started to hand over my controller.

"Take mine," the eldest said to his brother, "I'm sure you'll beat Dad, too."

Four-Letter Words

When I was a boy, I was strictly prohibited from uttering certain four-letter words. While they were banned from my home, I learned these words from my meticulous study of the bathroom stalls at the end of the fifth-grade hallway.

My childhood home, however, seemed cursed by a different, four-letter word that my parents used all the freaking time—*wait.*

I had to wait for Christmas and wait for my birthday. I had to wait for Saturday morning to watch cartoons. I had to wait for the final bell to be released from school. I had to wait for summer break and wait for the pool to open . . . only to wait some more for the lifeguards to finish their break so I could swim! Every Sunday, I was forced to wait in the pew for church to end, then wait at the dining table for everyone else to finish their lunch.

Ginny recently told me that the worst wait of her childhood occurred when a friend would phone and invite her to a playdate. While jumping up and down, she'd ask permission from her mom, who would often reply, "Let me think about it." This delay was torture to my favorite extrovert.

But now that we are parents, I can see the wisdom in waiting to make up one's mind.

When one of our children asks for something, my initial response is often, "No." Why do I have this reflexive denial? Maybe my kid has had a truly bad idea like when my six-year-old wanted my car keys to drive down the street to his friend's house.

Much more often, their request is innocuous. My impulse is to deny it because it's new or unplanned. There are times when my nip-it-in-the-bud response has more to do with the reality that I'm distracted or worried about something else. If I'd only give it a minute or two, I might find I'm better able to consider their ask on its own terms. I still might say "No," but at least I'd have a more thoughtful reason than an exasperated, "Because I said so! And, no, you may *not* go ask your mother!"

I also think that waiting helps my kids to develop character. I realize that I say "develop character" too often, for my six-year-old recently explained to his four-year-old sister that the phrase meant "do something we're not going to like."

So many things in our modern lives are instantaneous and on demand. But in the ancient language of Hebrew, "to wait" was synonymous with "to hope." Waiting is not merely about patience but faith. Waiting can sharpen a sense of attentiveness, and attentiveness, claimed the wise poet Mary Oliver, is the beginning of prayer.

The Bible *and* Mary Oliver. I'm really trying to bring home this point!

After church was (finally) over the other Sunday, my aforementioned four-year-old asked me to drive her for ice cream. I was already tired, but rather than squashing the idea, I told her I'd "think about it." She frowned, but sat down next to me on our front step to wait for my final answer. The sun was out after a cold, winter morning and its light wrapped my upturned face like a warm towel at a spa. Sleepily, I told my daughter that the ice cream truck would soon drive through the neighborhood. By "soon" I meant a couple of months when it was spring, but she demanded to know if the truck would come *today*!

"No," I admitted, "We'll have to wait for it."

To which she calmly replied, "Damn it."

Holy Shit

ON THE DRIVE HOME from a day at summer camp, my sons, ages nine and six, reported that they had learned the S-word. In the rearview mirror, I caught the conspiratorial look they exchanged—they were getting quite the education at this camp. Two days ago, the older brother declared the B-word was "bench."

But they correctly named the S-word. Then, they waited with bated breath to see how I would respond.

I asked them if they knew what this word meant. They did not. I told them it meant poop. Unlike the B-word, it was not something you would want to sit on! (I thought I was hilarious.)

I don't remember if Ginny and I made a conscious decision to say "poop" around our kids or if we just fell into it . . . yeesh, I should stop with the puns. My parents taught my younger brother and me to say "BM" for bowel movement. But everybody poops in our household. The term has *stuck*. (Why can't I stop? Probably because I'm writing about poop!)

When our first son was born, I learned a new word—meconium, which is the tar-like poop of a newborn. His first effort was handled by a labor and delivery nurse named Rhonda who wiped and rediapered that baby with Poop Olympic record speed. I was awed and immediately thought of her as the Great Rhonda. My son didn't have a chance to cry—he was swaddled and lying on his back before he knew what had happened!

When the next time came, I took my first turn. Though I must have emptied a bag of wipes, I still got meconium on his bare chest and my shirt and pants. My boy's howls peeled paint off the walls.

"You'll get better with practice," the Great Rhonda assured me. Exchanging a knowing look with Ginny, she added, "And you will practice. *Right*?"

Yes, ma'am!

I actually came to enjoy diaper changing time. I'd sing silly songs in my best Bob Dylan nasally voice. My kids would really giggle when I tickled their necks with my nose. I inhaled their laughter. Even the actual smell of poop wasn't that bad . . . except on the occasion when something had crawled up their butts and died!

The first poop in the potty is a big deal . . . for parents! Ginny and I didn't institute a reward system, although M&Ms were involved in both of our childhoods. Still, I felt triumphant when each of our kids got it down. (I cannot help myself.)

But even when they started having success on the toilet, I also felt sadness. They really do grow up so fast. One day, they're on the changing table, babbling "Da-da" and then, they are cursing at you from the backseat.

These days, my dispensing of the waste of others is restricted to our dog, which involves biodegradable plastic baggies. Our puppy is named Ramona after our favorite literary hero. I find it telling that Beverly Cleary never narrated poop in her novels. To my recollection, the only bathroom scenes involved Ramona the person locking Ribsy the dog behind the door and squeezing a whole tube of toothpaste in the sink. Cleary wrote in the mid-twentieth century when an entire generation of fathers never changed a diaper and never endured anything like the admonition of the Great Rhonda.

Times change. It's like I told my boys that day on the drive home from camp: context is everything. The S-word just means poop, but it is not always an appropriate time to use such language.

"Is now a good time, Dad?"

The three of us cursed and laughed all the way home.

The Laws of Laundry

The First Law of Laundry is that clothes will not fold themselves; objects at rest in the dryer, stay in the dryer.

I grumble about the chore, I admit. With three kids, the laundry is never-ending. Though there are three years between them, my two sons are now close in height; I have to double-check the sizes of their pants to sort into the correct pile. Some of my younger son's shirts were originally his brother's. This can also slow me down because I remember when the elder wore them. How can he have outgrown them already?

My daughter's clothes are easier to recognize. But there are a couple of T-shirts passed down all the way to her, mostly for sentimental reasons, like the tie-dye from the Montreat Conference Center in the Blue Ridge Mountains—a place sacred to both her parents.

This brings me to the Second Law of Laundry: clothes exert an equal and opposite force on you. You may find that you just can't get rid of a particular shirt.

After I finish folding and sorting all my kids' clothes, I lug them upstairs to put away in their rooms. Sometimes Ginny and I ask our offspring to do this for themselves. They groan when it's time to put away their clothes or pick up their toys.

But I tell my kids that, according to the laws of thermodynamics, your playroom will spiral into chaos if left on its own.

Life as a parent involves a lot of chores, which eat up hours upon hours. But though certain afternoons drag on, the years have flown by. You don't have to be Einstein to know that time is relative. I don't want to take this time in my life for granted.

How do we best spend our days? What will we notice? Who do we value? These are religious questions, but the answers aren't necessarily idealistic or dogmatic. Thomas Merton, the Trappist monk and prolific author, once said that he judged a monk's faithfulness not by how he prayed in the chapel, but by how he swept the floor of the common dining room. Willing, even joyful, obedience in service to others is a fundamental law in many religions and worldviews. Faithfulness may be measured by one's attention to the chore or task at hand.

The Third Law of Laundry is that there will be at least one extra sock in every load. I don't know why this is true. Maybe there is a scientific explanation. Maybe the dryer eats them for dessert.

But my research proves that there's no law in laundry against having fun—this extra sock makes a "handy" (Dad pun alert!) puppet that likes to tickle children!

The Warm Shivers

OF COURSE, EVERYTHING IS mere prelude to the Great Candy Day on October 31. But my family has a ritual in the weeks leading up to Halloween. While I load the dishwasher after supper, Ginny runs our kids through the bath and into their jammies. There's usually a Halloween cookie or two for them to grab as they scamper out the door in bare feet to our minivan parked outside. Once buckled, the sight-seeing of the neighborhood Halloween decorations begins.

Not all Halloween decorations are the same. While I hang a couple of ghosts from the porch, certain neighbors transform their front lawns into fake graveyards complete with smoke machines and zombies coming out of the grass. The more elaborate light displays are timed to music like "Ghostbusters" and ACDC's "Highway to Hell" playing on select FM radio channels.

For my kids, however, nothing is more impressive than the inflatables. These blow-up figures can be two stories tall. They light up and even move. The huge, red-eyed spider snaps its jaws!

I actually prefer the inflatables that my ten-year-old dismisses as "lame," like the Minions. Or Snoopy and the Peanuts gang. My son is on the lookout for scary stuff. I've already mentioned the spider. There is Dracula, baring his fangs, and the hooded Grim Reaper, waving his scythe. I ease the minivan close to the curb so that he and his younger siblings can get the "warm shivers"—what childhood author Arnold Lobel named as that lovely feeling of being scared when you know you are safe with your loved ones.

I also keep an eye on the clock. If we stay out too late, we risk the parent's nightmare of kids turning into grumpy monsters the next morning.

But it's hard for me to resist their pleas to keep driving. Ginny doesn't protest as I turn the minivan around one more time. Teenage parties and dating are still a long way down the road. If only for a little drive, I can pretend that most scary things are make-believe. I can't make time last.

I can make it count.

There's a house at the end of a cul-de-sac with two giant, inflatable eyeballs on the roof. As the kids squeal with delight, I look in the rearview mirror to catch a glimpse of their joy.

Section 2: **Little Big Moments When You Are Not Alone**

One of the Best Men I Know

ONE OF THE BEST men I know gazed at Orion in the sky this morning. Since his wife died, he has carried his coffee outside and looked for the famous constellation. It comforts him to know that some things remain the same.

His wife recently died of a progressive neurological disorder similar to ALS or Lou Gehrig's disease. She slowly lost her ability to move her body. And one of the best men I know cared for her every day.

The two of them raised two sons and used to be active outdoors—hiking, canoeing, camping. She first wondered if there was something wrong with her health after she fell repeatedly on a mountain trail. I knew her only in the last couple of years when she used a walker, then a motorized wheelchair. One of the best men I know was by her side no matter what.

The last six months of her life were especially hard. I could see the weariness of caregiving on his face. It is said that, in order to take care of themselves, full-time caregivers would need thirty-six hours in a day. It's impossible.

But one of the best men I know remained faithful to the promise he had made over forty years ago. He had promised to love her in sickness and in health until death.

He plays guitar and, like me, is a Bob Dylan fan. This morning, as I stared up at Orion between sips of my coffee, I whispered Dylan's lyrics as a prayer for him: "Nothing else can touch the beauty that I remember in my true love's eyes."

Maybe you've known someone with a progressive neurological disease. To lose control of your body with your mind still intact is a torturous way to die. But there can be moments of levity, even joy. That's what one of the best men I know said to me. A few weeks before she died, his wife told him through her computer's speech software that she had figured out a way for him to get a break from caring for her—she was going to start dating again! How they had laughed!

Orion was shining brightly this morning as I chuckled at this memory. All of the constellations have mythical origins. It's part of the human condition to ascribe fantastic stories to the great wonders above, like the sun, the moon, the stars.

Yet, I have seen wonders right here on earth—selfless devotion, grace under duress, cathartic laughter. And the greatest wonder of all is love. Just look at one of the best men I know.

Just Roll with It

My family went to the beach for our kids' spring break, the same little island where my wife has vacationed her entire life, with its roller-skating rink that predates her by another thirty years. The rink shows its age: a register that accepts cash only, a stereo with a cassette deck, and no air conditioning. No AC in eastern North Carolina! Despite the heat and humidity, countless folks have wheeled across the worn floors over the years. Now, my kids can say the same.

And it turned out that they were not the only first-timers the day we went.

He caught my attention when he ducked through the door. He was easily six feet, six inches tall. Well over three hundred pounds. His bushy red beard hung down his barrel chest. His cutoff T-shirt exposed tattoos on his hulking, sunburned arms. The proprietor fitted him with a pair of skates larger than electric cars.

I wondered if he was actually quite graceful. I tried to picture him executing a tight spin, one massive leg in the air behind him.

But as soon as this giant man had laced up and got to his feet, one skate went south and the other north. He managed to keep from falling by grabbing onto the railing.

"Whoa!" he boomed. "Not as easy as it looks!"

Now remember, I was with my young children who were also first-timers. As much as I hated to pry my eyes away, I had other responsibilities. I was tracking down my kids when the floor shook. You guessed it—timber! Big Man was down like a fallen tree.

I watched as three men whizzed up to where he lay prostrate on the floor. Two of them got their hands under his arms while the third man grabbed both his hands. Working together, they managed to pull Big Man back on his skates. By that point, I had rolled close enough to overhear them.

"I just can't," Big Man panted. "I ain't no good."

"Hey, don't give up!" one of the men smiled. "How 'bout I hold your hand?"

The familiar opening to the song "Hotel California" filled the air as they slowly skated away, hand in hand. Those two were about as mismatched a skating pair as you could ever hope to see: one wobbly and unsure, one strong and steady; one huge and hairy, one slim and trim; one white, one Black. But both were wearing the same bright smile, rolling along together.

I smiled, too, with hope.

Four Snapshots of Gratitude from a Beach Vacation

1

AFTER HITTING THE BEACH that first morning of our family vacation, I played UNO back at the house with my sons, their hair still wet from the ocean. I would have preferred for one of them to win, but the cards fell in my favor. Unfazed, my boys scampered off on their own, leaving me at the table with the deck of cards, shuffling through memories of my childhood. How I hated to lose at their age! I was not above cheating—I beat my father at Old Maid by looking at the reflection of the cards in his glasses!

There was a trip several decades ago to a different beach when my grandparents invited me to play Rook for the first time. It is a bidding game, like Spades, and the strategy was over my head. I must have been a liability to my partner. Yet, I only remembered the patience and kindness of the adults.

My younger son interrupted these thoughts by asking if we could play again. And I excitedly dealt the cards.

2

The next day I jogged to the end of the beach where the ocean met the sound. This was a short distance from where the rest of my family had set up on the sand, but it still felt like a slog. I had not been running in months, preferring to meander through the woods with our new dog, a form of exercise good for my soul but not for raising my heart rate.

I plodded underneath the hot sun, paying more attention to my aching legs and ragged breath than to the swimmers, sunbathers, or seagulls, when suddenly a small boy came out of nowhere and started running beside me. He caught my eye and, flashing a wild grin, the boy shot ahead down the beach! Not to be outdone, I managed to summon my own burst of speed. When I caught up to the child, he and I laughed as we both slowed down.

From behind, I heard, "Andrew!" He and I stopped. We shared the same name! While the little Andrew raced full speed back to his mom, I continued down the beach to my own family. Only I felt a little lighter.

3

I slipped off to the grocery store after breakfast. With eleven people in our extended family vacationing together, including five kids, preparing the meals felt like being a short-order cook. I had looked forward to a half-hour or so of quiet time in the car.

But as the wheels carried me down the road, my mind spun to various worries, some of which were real, others merely imagined.

I filled my grocery cart with fruit, coffee, milk, and the fixin's for tacos later that evening. I unloaded the items onto the conveyor belt. The man bagging groceries asked how I was doing and, still distracted, I mumbled, "Fine."

"That's good," came the bagger's reply. "It's a great day to be in the moment."

I stared at the man, his neatly trimmed white beard, his twinkling brown eyes. Who says such a thing? In a checkout line of all places? Who was this man? A saint?

Later that morning, I stood in the salty surf, holding my young daughter's hand as she squealed with delight.

4

My baby nephew cried in the middle of the night. I awoke, remembering what it was like when my kids were that young. My heart went out to my nephew's parents, particularly his mom.

Then, I checked on Ginny lying next to me. She was sound asleep. I grinned in the dark; she had earned it.

The Top Ten Back-to-School Advice from Dogs

1. Be excited! New class, new teacher, new friends, new school supplies, new collar, I mean, new clothes—it's all wonderful! Don't be afraid to hang your tongue out and shake your behind!

2. Be curious! Your nose is not as good as a dog's sniffer, but you can still investigate and explore your surroundings. Be on the hunt for new ideas!

3. Listen when you are told to "Sit!" (and obey other commands, too). You may not understand why, but the adult instructing you has the bigger picture in mind and your best interest at heart. So, listen to what you are told and . . .

4. Play when you can! When you get the chance to go outside, romp in the sunshine! Roll around in the grass! Fetch the ball! Chase squirrels! (But leave the mail carrier alone. Seriously.)

5. Know that things might not always seem fair. Why does the cat nap on the bed and use the bathroom inside? It might seem like a double standard, but adults know what they are doing (see No. 3). Comparison is the thief of joy, so be cautious about judging someone else's experience. After all, the cat doesn't have the joy of rolling on the dead squirrel in the road!

6. Eat snacks, snacks, and more snacks. Woof 'em up!

7. Speak up! Do you need to go to the bathroom? Then whine at the door! (Or, maybe raise your hand.) Teachers and other staff are there to help you. You don't have a tail to put between your legs, but if you are scared or hurt, use your words to let someone know.

8. Trust that your family will always come back. The people you live with will go somewhere else to do unexplainable things with computers or commuters or something like that. Once again, you don't always know why. But know this: you will see them again . . . and they come back with snacks!

9. Make friends of all shapes, sizes, and colors. If a Lab can be buds with a poodle, and a Great Dane can chill out with a Chihuahua, then you can make friends with kids who don't look like you. Maybe even best friends.

10. And finally, when you meet someone new, sniff their rear end!

Okay, maybe not all advice from dogs is to be followed exactly, but you get the idea. Take it from Robert Benchley, a newspaper columnist more famous than me: "A child can learn a lot from a dog: obedience, loyalty, and the importance of turning around three times before lying down."

A Shimmer in a Fifth-Grade Hallway

I LEARNED HOW TO tell the time in elementary school, a skill that I practice multiple times every single day. Other lessons I use less frequently but still cheerfully: I sing the alphabet under my breath while searching the library stacks and recite a rhyme to figure out how many days are in certain months. And I could never forget my old friend Roy G. Biv for naming the colors of the rainbow!

But most of what I learned was, as the great Mister Rogers put it, "caught, not taught," referring to what was modeled for me by teachers, staff, and fellow students. There is one moment that stands out in my mind like the bright full moon above the morning's horizon.

Fifth grade, spring semester. When walking to recess with the rest of the class, a boy held hands with a girl. One moment, they were just strolling along like the rest of us, the next he reached for her hand, and she reached for his. I saw this happen mere feet in front of me and the moment they touched sent shock waves up my spine! We were no longer merely heading to play basketball but into the great unknown—a thrilling and terrifying future that would include proms, tuxedos, and boutonnières. Stomach butterflies, first kisses, and broken hearts. Yes, the journey from childhood through adolescence was still a long, winding road with countless steps and missteps, not to mention awkward moments.

But something changed right there at that moment in the hallway.

There's something here that I wish to catch and hold even now, thirty years later. Something bigger and more sacred than any idealized notion of romance or childhood or innocence. Something about how people of any age can reach for each other in reciprocal, life-giving ways.

I've learned how the word "manipulate" is derived from the Latin for hand. I've seen enough of the ways that adults use their bodies and words to coerce, pressure, intimidate, and belittle. Such abuse is also caught, not taught—replicated in families and family systems, including communities of worship. It's hard, painful, and holy to name these abuses and work for reconciliation with the truth held firmly before us.

Yet, our hands are also capable of language beyond words. We say more with a hand on someone's shoulder than any sermon. Our hands are like stars, and we give light with each gentle, caring touch. I saw one such shimmer that afternoon thirty years ago in the fifth-grade hallway. He reached for her hand, and she reached for his. Together they walked down the hall toward the bright day that streamed through the open doors.

A James Taylor Remix about Parenting

"Deep greens and blues are the colors I choose," sings James Taylor, a line that often plays in my mind in North Carolina in April. Though Taylor was born in Boston, his family moved to Chapel Hill when he was three years old. By his early twenties, he had made a name for himself as a singer-songwriter. In April 2003, the bridge over Morgan Creek, which is only a couple miles from his childhood home, was renamed after him.

And in April 2023, my wife's minivan broke down on the same bridge.

"All you gotta do is call, and I'll be there . . . "

Except when, as we had planned earlier that day, I'm already in line to pick up our three kids after school!

Since I couldn't pick up Ginny from the bridge myself, I phoned our friend, who was happy to arrange for his wife to help her. While she was waiting with our minivan, nearby construction workers helped her unload the groceries from the trunk. The tow truck arrived in record time.

"Things are gonna work out fine . . . "

Though a six-time Grammy Award winner, Taylor admits that he neither reads nor writes music. Instead, he "wanders" around on his guitar, picking notes until he discovers something that sounds good. This meandering is actually part of his creative method: "Songwriting is too mysterious and uncontrolled a process for me to direct it toward any one thing."

Parenting is also a wandering improvisation. Sure, Ginny and I make plans. We have a family calendar (although sometimes half a month has passed before we fill it out). But schedules change, occasionally fall apart. There is strep throat in the preschool, the dog gets sick on the carpet, an oil leak ruins the alternator.

"Won't you look down upon me, Jesus!"

"I don't know much about God," Taylor claimed in another interview, "but if everything does originate with God, then certainly songs do as well." I'd add tow trucks, cleaning supplies, and your village of support that helps you raise your children.

That afternoon, the kids and I returned from school. As they ran into the house, slinging their backpacks on the floor, I took a deep breath. An unexpected change in plans is stressful, yet also can be an occasion for gratitude. I have three healthy kids, a dog that greets me at the door, a little money in my checking account, and a life shared with the loveliest person I know. A few minutes later, she was home.

"Whenever I see your smiling face, I have to smile myself."

A Royal Pain in Public

I DON'T MAKE MUCH of an effort to follow the Royal Family of England. But even I saw the photos of Prince Louis of Cambridge at the Queen's Platinum Jubilee.

As the world paid tribute to Her Majesty, Queen Elizabeth II, one of her great-grandchildren was a bit "cheeky," as they say across the pond. Prince Louis covered his ears and screamed. He stuck his tongue out at his mother and blew a raspberry. I was like, hey, don't I know that kid?

Royal or not, four-year-old kids act like they are four years old. This should not be a news flash!

What was surprising—actually, infuriating—was the criticism levied at the aforementioned mother, Kate Middleton, the Duchess of Cambridge. Here is a sampling from social media:

"Kate had better get it together as a parent."

"That boy is not getting any discipline at home."

"Wow, Kate, you have no control of your children."

Crikey!

I appreciated the take by Kerri Sackville, a columnist for *The Sydney Morning Herald*: "You know who doesn't judge others for their parenting? Those of us who know how hard it is."

I love my three kids. Ginny and I waited a long time for them, and for a few agonizing years, we feared that our dream of parenthood was never to be. There are times when I am so overwhelmed with gratitude for the miracle of my children's existence that my eyes brim with tears.

This usually happens when my kids are asleep.

During my waking hours, I sometimes cry for other reasons. Frustration. Impatience. Borderline despair: "My God, will you ever get your shoes on? How many times do I have to tell you?!?!"

I have a four-year-old. Recently, she had a meltdown in church. The same church where I happened to be preaching. If television cameras had been tuned onto my face, I assure you that I would not have been as unflappable as the Duchess of Cambridge!

Jason Gay, sportswriter for *The Wall Street Journal*, writes that, when he encounters a parent attempting to alleviate a child's tantrum, "I have no urge to give that parent unsolicited advice. I want to give that parent a beer. Or three beers."

In my particular case, maybe a strong pour from that holy wine.

Last week, my four-year-old tore around a minor league baseball stadium like a banshee on a sugar high. She accidently bumped an older gentleman, causing him to slosh a little of his beer on his shirt! I quickly apologized. But he waved me off: "You've got your hands full. I remember what it was like."

To all of us laboring or "labouring" to raise children, I say cheers to that!

Open Letter to the Stranger Who Was Critical of My Parenting in the Grocery Store

Dear fellow shopper,

My name is Andrew. You don't know that because you didn't march up to me in the grocery store to introduce yourself. Though we had never met, you felt comfortable saying to me, "You will certainly spoil her!" after you had seen me give my daughter a food she demanded to have.

Whatever your intention was with your comment, I felt defensive, as I imagine you might have also felt when I snapped back, "She's not a gallon of milk!"

You rolled your eyes and pushed your cart away in a huff as I fumed by the produce section.

Clearly, you and I got off on the wrong foot. Now, with some time and distance on our side, how about we step back and take another look at what unfolded between us?

Ram Dass, a spiritual teacher and author, once characterized the "judgment mind" in this way: "We are constantly saying, 'You are too this, or I'm too this.'"

I'm curious—why do you think we judged each other so harshly? I wonder now if your reaction had more to do with you than with me. Was there a time when you, too, acquiesced to your kid's meltdown in the checkout line and gave her whatever would make her quiet, even if it was a piece of candy right before supper? Is there something about your now-grown child that has you fearing that you somehow "spoiled" her? Maybe my situation struck a little too close to home.

I admit that I can get a little defensive about my parenting choices. Ok, more than a little defensive. I'm not always sure what to do—when to be firm, when to simply move on. Candidly, my reaction depends, in part, on how I'm feeling, upon whether or not I've had a productive day or enough sleep the night before. I'm not as consistent a parent as I would like to be.

I don't know if our paths will ever cross again, but I wish to give you the benefit of the doubt. I'm sure you have stories to share. Maybe you have gleaned wisdom from your experience that really could help me the next time my daughter wants that box of sugary cereal. It would also help me to hear about your trials and errors, if only to know that I'm not alone in my frustrations and doubts. Who knows? We might even end up laughing together!

But before I could have been open to receiving your hard-won advice, I would have needed to know first that you were on my side. That you understood how hard it is and wanted to help. That you were willing to hold space in that uncomfortable parenting moment not with judgment but with empathy. Next time, could you suspend your impulse to criticize? Even if my kid is throwing an ear-piercing, head-splitting tantrum? Maybe instead lend a helping hand? Maybe help to unload the shopping cart in the checkout line?

Here's the truth: just a sympathetic smile from you would have meant a great deal to me. I bet you know that. After all, one of the gifts of parenthood is that it can teach us to appreciate the small things that loom large in our hearts.

Ram Dass also wrote, "We are all just walking each other home."

While you and I parted ways, our encounter has stayed with me. Instead of saying, "You're too this," or "I'm too that," I hope we could learn from it. Kindness is one thing that we can always give to one another. And what could ever be a more eloquent prayer than that?

In hope,

Andrew

Hope in Jeopardy

My three children woke up to less than half an inch of snow. "A dusting," I called it, peering over their heads into the backyard. They looked at the same scene and made a different assessment: "It snowed enough to go sledding!"

I like to think of myself as a glass-half-full guy. But a dusting is still a dusting.

Earlier that week, I had read a piece in *The New York Times* on Amy Schneider, the recent winner of forty consecutive contests on the game show *Jeopardy!* That's the most wins ever by a woman. The article highlighted Schneider's experience with religion. Though she's now an atheist, a religious experience left a lasting impression on her.

Raised in the Roman Catholic Church, Schneider had moved away from the faith by 2002. Yet, she agreed to attend an event featuring Pope John Paul II to appease her mother. She and her family had to wait overnight to ensure their seats. But they neglected to bring tents or any camping equipment. That was bad enough. Then, it started to rain.

To this day, Schneider claims, "Whenever it gets bad, I think, 'I'm not lying in a field in the rain.'"

That attitude is not exactly the same as a glass half full. But the thought that "it could be worse" can lead to looking at a negative situation more favorably. Schneider was inspired to try new things: "I'll give anything a shot now."

I thought of Schneider that particular morning when, just as I feared, the dusting of snow was good for only two-and-a-half sled rides down our neighborhood hill. Keep in mind that I have three children. Frustration mounted and the sledders began to turn on each other. What should I do? What would Schneider do?

I'll take "Fun Things To Do on a Hill" for $200.

Answer: What is rolling downhill?

I'm happy to report I had three happy contestants.

To be clear, I am not judging Schneider for leaving organized religion. As a pastor, I am painfully aware that the church is often its own worst enemy. Terrible things have been done in the name of God—things much worse than enduring a cold night in the rain. I'm not naïve.

But I am hopeful. My friend and colleague MaryAnn McKibben Dana wrote that hope, unlike mere optimism, "demands that we do something with it." Certainly, there are negative situations in life. However, much of our response depends on how we look at a situation, then how we react. That particular morning, there was only a dusting of snow, yet while the sledding situation put the prospect of fun in jeopardy, we did something else. And the experience turned out to be full—full of joy and mugs full of hot chocolate waiting for us back home.

Thank You, Sir!

A DOZEN STUDENTS BOWED to the flag, then turned and bowed again to their instructor, shouting, "Thank you, sir!" Every tae kwon do class begins and ends in this manner.

But after this class, my son's instructor walked purposefully over and shook my hand. "When will I see you on the mat with other adults?" He smiled. "I can tell you're interested. I can see it in your eyes."

This instructor doesn't miss much, but he did misinterpret my focused attention on that particular workout. While I have no desire to learn tae kwon do, I profess a deep appreciation for what I saw being taught to the students.

It's true that today's children have certain advantages over previous generations. Technology affords opportunities never before imagined. With gains in racial and gender equity, more children and youth are free(er) to be their true selves.

And, as Dr. Becky Kennedy, a popular child clinical psychologist, puts it, two things are true: it's also hard to be a kid in today's culture. According to a study by scholars at the universities of Florida and Denver, 60 percent of parents with children aged 14 to 18 reported cyberbullying in 2020, which is up from 32 percent in 2007. Following the COVID-19 pandemic and social isolation, numerous studies have shown that children's mental health has suffered, including lowered self-esteem. The reasons for these struggles are multifaceted; the problems are complex.

I have seen how part of a healthy solution may be as simple as breaking a wooden board.

My son wanted to take tae kwon do so that he could break a board in two. Having no previous experience with martial arts, I tried to manage his expectations, assuming that splitting anything with your appendage was an advanced technique and thus required time to learn.

What do I know? On his second day of class, the instructor called my son to the front of the room, then my boy broke a board in half with his fist! My son was wearing a facemask, but I could tell by his eyes that he grinned from ear to ear!

While every student has this affirming experience on the second day of class, tae kwon do is about much more than breaking boards. As is true of any sport or athletic endeavor, certain skills do not come quickly or easily, especially intangible lessons like perseverance and commitment. As Mister Rogers claimed, those lessons are "caught, not taught." They are modeled for children who are then encouraged and inspired to do the same.

Not many paragraphs mention both Mister Rogers and martial arts! But back to my conversation with the tae kwon do instructor . . .

The afternoon in which the instructor misread the look in my eyes, I had just watched a student struggle through a particular drill. It was clear from where I sat that this child was frustrated and wanted to quit. The instructor pushed him, but without shaming him in front of the others. Instead, the rest of the class encouraged their fellow student with cheers! When the struggling student finished the drill, their applause was just as loud as when someone else broke their first board. This child wore an unmistakable look of pride. Somewhere, Mister Rogers smiled, too.

Tae kwon do will remain my son's thing, not mine. But I add my "Thank you, sir" out of deep respect for adults who inspire young people to learn values from athletics and, along the way, teach them even more about themselves.

Soccer Skills

I have tried to get into football. Not the old American pigskin, but the international version played at the 2022 World Cup in Qatar. It's a struggle for me.

I did not play the game as a child or youth. I knew soccer players, but they tended to keep to their tribe. I assumed they bonded over their love of running and other such activities. Maybe sticking forks in their eyes?

I was a baseball player. My teammates and I would groan when our coach asked us to run to the outfield fence and back. One gains an insightful perspective about the difference between these two sports by comparing umpires—generally speaking, soccer referees look like they have just completed a triathlon, while your typical baseball umpire looks as though he has just completed a third run through the all-you-can-eat buffet.

Admittedly, baseball is no longer America's pastime. The sport is so less popular than football and basketball that it is vying for attention with soccer . . . of all things! Major League Baseball has now resorted to imposing time limits between pitches to speed up the games and appeal to younger generations.

But fans like me know that players, coaches, and umps are not merely spitting in the dirt between pitches. Baseball is a game of strategic thinking—deciding where the infielders are positioned, the type of pitch to throw, and the toppings for hotdogs.

From my limited World Cup research (I keep dozing off in front of the TV), soccer strategy involves somebody kicking the ball down the sidelines, then someone else kicking the ball to the center of the field, and finally somebody trying to kick it in the goal. The point seems to be to run as fast and far as you can for as long and hard as you can.

There must be more strategy! Surely, soccer fans could enlighten me just as I might regale them about the back door curveball, sacrifice bunt, or hotdog relish.

I emailed a high school friend who, other than his love of soccer, is a perfectly reasonable guy. He explained that the strategy was to kick the ball down the sidelines, then kick the ball to the center of the field, and finally to try to kick it in the goal. The point was to run as fast and far as you can for as long and hard as you can.

I would rather stick a fork in my eye.

My son and I tried to watch the paint dry that was this year's match between the U.S.A. and England. Later, he asked me about the result—of the game, not my nap. I told him it ended in a tie. He looked blankly at me. Zero to zero, I added.

"But Dad, who won?"

Maybe not everything has to be win or lose. I don't have to compare sports to each other. They can just be different and unique. Neither better nor worse.

If you need me, I'll be waiting for spring over here with the mustard and relish. No forks required.

Murmuration

My family arrived at the soccer field early. First-time jitters. I was surprised that a half-dozen families had already congregated along the chain-link fence. As I lugged our camping chairs across the parking lot, I noticed that other parents had brought snacks. Brilliant! Why hadn't I thought of that?

Our four-year-old daughter rushed ahead with her brand new, shiny soccer ball to a huddle of her fellow tiny kickers. She is one to take the ball and run with it in more ways than one.

As more minivans pulled into the parking lot, there were soon dozens of kids milling about in their uniforms, shin guards, and cleats. My oldest son asked, "Dad, when does this thing start?"

"Any minute now," I assured him. But we continued to wait. And wait.

Finally, a high-pitched whistle split the air. Tiny kickers froze. Conversations stopped. All eyes turned toward the man who had whistled with his two fingers in his mouth.

"So, is anybody here the coach?"

Silence.

Then, the crowds began to murmur: *No coach? Really? What the . . .* Ginny checked her email. How could this have happened?

Another whistle.

"Well, I'm not the coach. But let's get the kids on the field!"

It turned out that we just needed marching orders! At his command, the long-legged caregivers sprang into action, herding their tiny kickers through the gate.

"Daddy, will you come with me?" Suddenly, my daughter seemed so small.

Other than elementary school recess, I have no experience playing the "other" football game. Ginny, however, had set the single season scoring record at her high school—as a freshman! By all rights, she should have been on the field. But parenting is a team game, and she was being double-teamed by our hungry boys. Why hadn't I thought to bring snacks?

An email would confirm that the coaches had called off practice due to the water-logged condition of the field. My daughter and I squished our way across the grass. Along with many others, I looked to the whistler for direction.

As if reading our minds, he shrugged. "Don't look at me. I coach baseball."

Thank God for the soccer moms. They divided the kids into three groups. My daughter's impromptu instructor told the young players to dribble their ball down the white line that was spray-painted on the field.

Normally a headlong kind of girl, my daughter tentatively kicked the ball a few times, then bent down to pick it up and put it back on the line. Perhaps she thought that was the technique. Maybe she was nervous at her first practice.

When kids began to pile up behind her, the soccer mom gently directed them to go around. My daughter's face fell. She took off running across the field and through the gate. By the parking lot, she plopped down and began pulling off her cleats.

This was not going well.

I often feel lost as a parent. My kids and I rarely follow the best-laid plans like a straight line. This can be frustrating and stressful. But we can also make things up as we go along. Forced to wing it, my family can embrace the present as a gift. Maybe we don't have a clear sense of direction or marching orders, but maybe we can find a new way.

As Ginny consoled our daughter, our sons started kicking a ball around with some older kids. Their laughter cheered me. I looked back in the direction of the parking lot and saw Ginny helping our daughter lace up her cleats. Our tiny kicker rejoined her tribe on the field in time for the scrimmage—atta-girl!

Ginny then stood beside me to watch. No one on the field seemed to know what team they were on. The kids chased the ball in mass like a flock of starlings. I know next to nothing about soccer, but I know that this pulsating formation of birds, which moves as if it is one body, is called a murmuration.

When first married, Ginny and I would stroll together after supper in the small park beside our graduate school apartments and watch the murmuration soar in the twilight. Only recently out of the nest and learning to fly on our own, we dreamed about having kids one day.

Now cheering for our daughter, I was feeling pretty good about our first soccer experience. Until I felt the tug on the leg of my pants.

"Dad, why didn't you bring snacks?"

Unicorn Biscuit Head

A RIDDLE: WHY DOES a young child want to play a sport?

I'll give you a hint: the answer rhymes with "run"—not "develop character."

Here's another hint by way of a story:

On a warm spring day long, long ago—about last Tuesday—a group of five- and six-year-olds scuttled onto a grassy field and surrounded their two soccer coaches like a scurry of squirrels around an oak tree. The coaches were smiling and already knew everyone's name.

The first thing the coaches did was to pass out red and blue "pinnies," which sparked debate among the youngsters, for these articles of clothing were neither pens nor pins nor made of pennies. For the smallest players, including my daughter, the nylon mesh was tied in the front like this was the 1980s. Pinnies on, they were ready to go!

The first game was a classic version of "Red Light, Green Light." Each player kicked a ball straight ahead (more or less) until a coach shouted, "Red light!" Then, the players were supposed to trap the ball with one of their feet. Many fell over in the grass, laughing. Some sat on the ball like it was an egg, an interpretation that came naturally because, as per the instructions, everyone flapped their arms and did the chicken dance whenever a coach shouted, "Yellow light!"

The next game was a variation of "Sharks and Minnows." I think the point was for the minnows to kick the half-dozen soccer balls to the other side of the field without letting the sharks kick them in the opposite direction. But the sharks and minnows promptly forgot the instructions, as well as their assigned roles, and spent the time kicking whichever ball in whatever direction while declaring what kind of animal they really wanted to be—alligators, crocodiles, sea snakes, tigers, eagles!

"I am a unicorn biscuit head!"

That's my girl! She didn't have the best experience playing last year on a different team. So it's a joy to watch her run and tumble and fall down laughing in the grass, and I'm grateful to her brilliant coaches for creating an environment where she can express herself in all of her unicorn-biscuit-headness. Because I know that, along the way, she'll also learn a little about soccer, and about being a good teammate, and about what it means to get up after she falls down. She'll develop character.

And the answer to the riddle is, of course, fun.

Really Real

First thing, they put down their baseball equipment in the dugout. Then, the seven-year-olds put on their batting gloves. They ask their coaches when they'll play in a real game.

They run a warmup sprint to the outfield fence. They practice spitting. They wear their hats backwards, forewords, sideways. More spitting practice. They ask again about playing in a real game.

They put on their helmets and pick up their bats. They rename their baseball helmets "marshmallows." They laugh uncontrollably. They take a few warmup swings, then they draw circles and polygons in the dirt with their bats. They make an X that marks a spot for treasure. They laugh some more.

They hit baseballs off batting tees. They hit the tees themselves. They spit and ask coaches about snacks. They ask coaches about playing in a real game.

They take off their batting gloves. They put away bats and helmets, I mean, marshmallows. They put on their fielding gloves and spit. They throw baseballs over the fence. They laugh and retrieve the balls. When they get back on the field, they ask about snacks.

During fielding practice, they hustle after balls that roll between their legs. They wear hats backwards, forewords, sideways. They throw and catch. They run and rest. They ask again about snacks. They take a water break and they spill water on each other. They laugh and laugh.

They run to help a teammate who's hit by an errant ball. They pat his shoulder. They get him laughing again. They invite each other to their birthday parties. They search for four-leaf clovers. They spit like pros. They ask about playing in a real game.

My son and his teammates have three more weeks until their first "real" game. But to my way of seeing things, what they're already doing is as real as it gets.

You Can't Be Serious

NORTH CAROLINA STATE SENATORS recently proposed a bill that youth sports "shall not include awards for participants based solely on their participation."

What a relief! I've been fretting about the wrong things getting into the hands of my children! How many times have I awoken in the night, dripping in a cold sweat, fearing for the lives of my loved ones because of a $5 trophy?!

But parents can now rest assured that their five-year-olds will not leave T-ball packing the heat of shiny, gold-plated hardware. As Jason Gay, sportswriter for *The Wall Street Journal*, put it, "If there's one thing that constituents want from their elected officials, it's a heavy regulatory hand in the youth sports trophy industry." Yes!

(Oh, wait; Gay was kidding?!)

The very same senators, mind you, recently passed a bill repealing laws for "pistol purchasing permits." Keep in mind that the law requiring background checks for the purchase of handguns had been on the books since 1919. But no more. Now, sheriffs won't have the authority to deny firearms to suspected dangerous people.

But we'll be damned if your tiny soccer player leaves the field with a participation trophy!

I have searched in vain for any hard evidence documenting the deleterious impacts of participation trophies on children. Of course, facts were not invited to participate in the passing of the bill about handgun permits.

Otherwise, our senators might think about how guns are the leading cause of death among children and teens here in North Carolina.

And how gun-related deaths were the single biggest contributor to the state's child mortality rate, rising by eleven percent from 2019 to 2021—the largest spike in the past fifty years.

"That really shows us," noted Dr. Steven Woolf, professor of population health and author of this study, "how many children are dying from preventable causes—these are manmade pathogens, not biological."

But then again, what does Dr. Woolf know? He only has the overwhelming majority of the medical community behind him.

Undaunted by appeals to reason deemed unpatriotic or "woke," our elected officials remain stalwart in the face of evidence. Their crusade against participation trophies is part of their American Dream: without having to pass out such trophies, more Americans can get their hands on a gun.

God help us. Seriously.

Bullets into Baseball Bats

On July 10, 2022, gunshots were fired at a Little League Baseball game in Wilson, North Carolina. You can find the video footage on Facebook, although I admit that I cannot watch—the near misses hit too close to home.

My six-year-old son just finished playing T-ball. I enjoy baseball, but the fun of this experience was more about the delightful kids than the actual sport. Multiple players preferred to wear their gloves on their heads. The shortstop lay on his back and made dirt angels with his arms and legs. Twin sisters only threw the ball to each other, no matter where they were positioned.

And there was Bubba.

His grandmother would holler, "Bubba, swing that bat!"

That bat was bigger than Bubba, but that didn't stop our little dynamo from swinging so hard that he spun in circles. Half the time, Bubba was so dizzy he took off toward third base instead of first!

After the last game, my son, his glove on his head, grinned: "Dad, I can't wait to play next year!"

As a parent, what more can you ask for? Sure, you might like your kid to learn a few fundamentals—maybe not the intricacies of a double play but how to wear the glove. At the end of the day, you just want kids to have fun and look forward to the next time.

There almost wasn't a next time for players and coaches in Wilson.

The list of places where children have been shot and murdered includes schools, movie theaters, and playgrounds. Guns were also fired at Little Leaguers in North Charleston, South Carolina. How do we even begin to address this evil?

My fellow pastor and father Chris Breslin was one of the coaches on the field in Wilson. Breslin posted to Facebook that, when he closes his eyes, he relives the horrific images of that day. Whizzing bullets. Parents huddled under the bleachers. The young boy who Breslin covered with his own body asked if they were going to die. This child added, "I'm never playing baseball again."

But as a person of faith, Breslin has another vision. He posted a friend's artwork that echoes the biblical Isaiah's vision of turning swords into plowshares; the artwork depicts a speeding bullet morphing into a metal baseball bat.

When I close my eyes, I can recall the metallic ping of Bubba's oversized bat making contact with the baseball. I can hear his grandmother's voice above the cheering fans, "The other way, Bubba! Run to first base!"

What sights and sounds will our children remember? How can we ensure that they are heading into the right direction in life?

How can we make sure there is a next season?

Breslin challenged all of us to take the next steps: "We must vote and harangue and persuade and partner to create a culture of action that is unsatisfied with anything less than justice, peace, and safety for our kids, for all kids, everywhere."

Unsatisfied with anything less than bullets into baseball bats.

A Sacrifice Drive

Growing up, my younger brother and I both played baseball. Since my brother moved to New York City more than a decade ago, my father and I have tried to meet him every summer at a different ballpark to watch a major league game. Over the years, the three of us have seen some great ones: A one-hitter pitched in Philadelphia. A ninth-inning rally in Cleveland. We have watched future Hall of Fame players like Derek Jeter and Chipper Jones.

But the most memorable moments have been the adventures we shared when our best-laid plans went awry: The rain delay in Chicago. The time the Metro was shut down in Washington. The midnight fire alarm in the hotel.

We have not traveled as much in recent years due to the births of our children and the COVID-19 pandemic. But not long ago, my brother visited our parents in Raleigh. We were excited to watch a baseball team much closer to home—the Durham Bulls. While minor league, the Bulls boasted the No. 1 prospect in baseball, a twenty-year-old power-hitting, slick-fielding short-stop named Wander Franco.

My brother carpooled with our father to the game while I drove from my home. They texted me while I was still heading north on U.S. Highway 15. They were already in their seats! I zipped into a parking space and hustled around the car to pay the parking meter. Stuffing the receipt in my pocket, I had a moment of confusion—where were my keys?

My heart sank.

I sprinted back to my car and saw my keys lying in the driver's seat. All the doors were locked. I could hear the national anthem playing in the stadium behind me. What was I going to do?

I did have my cell phone. I texted my brother first. Next, I called a roadside assistance company and was directed to an online request form. I texted my brother again. I hoped I wouldn't miss too much of the game.

He immediately called with a different idea. Come inside the ballpark. After a few innings, he and Dad would drive me to my house, then back to my car with the spare key.

Though we faced a long drive to my house and back, we wanted to stay long enough to watch Franco for a couple of at-bats. The young superstar did not disappoint. On his second trip to the plate, he smashed a home run over the centerfield fence!

The next time Franco came up to the plate, there were runners on second and third with no outs. Baseball fans know that a simple fly ball to the outfield will score the run. Though the hitter makes an out, it helps the team. For this reason, it's called a sacrifice fly.

But Franco swung for the fences again and tapped the ball weakly to third base. No runs scored.

While certainly a major league talent, Franco is still young. As part of his maturation, he must learn that sacrifice is the heart of this team game.

While I will remember locking my keys in the car, the memory I hold dear is of riding in the back seat of Dad's car, my brother driving through the night, and all three of us laughing. No one complained even once. Though I, too, tended to be self-centered as a young adult, I've learned over the years that love is sacrifice.

No Shame in Free Lunch

At the playground, I happened to hear a child describe her lunch that day as a "pizza in the shape of a rectangle." I caught her parent's eyes and shared a smile. I remembered that pizza from my childhood!

After classes went exclusively virtual due to the COVID-19 pandemic in the spring of 2020, federal funds provided counties the ability to offer meals on a "grab-and-go" basis in takeout containers. These meals were free to all students. My kids piled into our minivan on several occasions. They loved the hot rolls!

From masks to physical distancing, the following school years have continued to be different. But cafeterias still have a vital role. About one in four children in the county where I live suffers from food insecurity. Thankfully, schools help to meet their basic nutrition needs.

Free and reduced-price school meals have been an essential aspect of helping children and families for a long time. The National School Lunch Act was established in 1946 by President Harry Truman.

But now, thanks to The Universal School Meals Program Act of 2021, school lunches are free to all students—no more having to apply for the federally assisted meals program.

Why should this meal program be "universal" for all students?

Sadly, "lunch shaming" is almost as prevalent in schools as that rectangular pizza.

Shame can be served by school administrators who refuse to serve students if they owe money. But more often, shaming comes from fellow students.

Jennifer Anderson is a registered dietitian and founder of Kids Eat in Color, a blog and online resource that "specializes in feeding children and picky eating." Anderson is also sensitive to socioeconomic differences and designs weekly meal plans for families with fixed incomes or limited means.

On the Kids Eat in Color Facebook page, Anderson recently cited an example of an eight-year-old saying, "I don't think school lunches are very healthy." It is likely that this idea was served to the child at home.

Anderson disagrees: "School lunches protect millions of children's brains and bodies from hunger so that they can learn."

Rather than criticizing school lunches, parents can become involved with the PTA and work to include more locally sourced fresh food and vegetables on the menu.

But there is no excuse for stigmatizing this essential service. Missing meals can have a negative snowball effect on a child's health. As Anderson emphasizes, "You have no idea how one comment from an unhungry child to a child at risk of hunger can cause long-term damage."

The universal free meal program has been under fire from certain conservative groups. In a recent editorial, the Heritage Foundation declared free meals for all students was "notoriously wasteful." Yet, the authors failed to cite even a single statistic to support their claim. They have neither facts nor common sense on their side. Even if all meals were free, it stretches the bounds of credulity to assert that all students would participate.

But if the meals were universal, it could very well remove the stigma from those students who truly need the nutrition.

As Diane Pratt-Heavner, spokesperson for the School Nutrition Association, said, "When the meals are all free, there's no shame in taking one." Sounds delicious to me.

Getting It Right on Veterans Day

First, a list of what I've gotten wrong on Veterans Day.

On the morning of November 11, 2018, I hustled my kindergartner out the door and drove like mad only to find an empty school parking lot. Veterans Day has been a national holiday on November 11 since President Gerald Ford signed it into law in 1978. I was born in 1981. No excuse for forgetting!

I have misspelled the holiday. It is not written as Veteran's or Veterans' Day. There is no apostrophe because this day does not belong to a particular individual or group. Veterans Day is meant to recognize all living people who have served in the armed forces, including those who have fought in combat.

In previous years, I have also confused honoring the service of veterans with celebrating certain wars. There is no "good war"—this is a contradiction in terms. Many veterans would be the first to say that war is evil.

Many would also tell you that anyone who eagerly seeks war is a charlatan, a fool, or worse. Yet, I have succumbed to the allure of political rhetoric and eagerly marched to the drumbeat of war—from the safety of my own home, that is.

I've made plenty of mistakes, some out of carelessness, others from arrogance. So what have I gotten right?

I have tried to be someone a veteran could trust to listen and not to judge.

Many of the veterans I know are the hardest on themselves. They regret certain things they have done and other things left undone. They have witnessed brutalities that should not be printed. They have pain that words cannot express.

Without breaking their confidence, I will say that such stories about the horrors of war have made me shiver, though I had been drinking hot coffee at the time of the telling. And then these stories have kept me awake at night for longer than any dose of caffeine.

When veterans have shared their stories, I have mainly listened. I have offered words like "mercy" and "grace" and "God" in hopes that veterans will go gently between these words and find solace in the quiet of their own thoughts. What is right and holy about these words is not the person who shares them but the person who finds peace from them.

So here is what I would like to get right on Veterans Day and every day: All year long, each one of us can honor veterans by supporting their physical and emotional health upon their return from conflict, all the while summoning every bit of our energy, intelligence, imagination, and love to put an end to all wars. We honor the veterans in our community by working to ensure that no one has to leave to fight the next war.

Working for peace is always the right thing to do.

And don't forget to reach out to a veteran. On most days, it's not about having the right words to say but about offering listening support. And when you give your time and attention, please remember to get childcare. Your kid has the day off from school.

Dads at the Airport

AIRPORTS ARE CURIOUS VILLAGES. We are brought together only to leave. But that doesn't mean we can't notice and appreciate one another. Not only the employees who, God bless, have their hands full, but also our fellow flyers. I'm looking at the dads.

There was a father at the baggage check who somehow managed to lift the bulky family suitcase onto the scale and present all the necessary documents from the recesses of his fanny pack, all while a little boy clung to each of his legs.

There was the dad with triplets—count them!—who re-looped three belts around three tiny waists after passing through security. Sure, you might suggest different pants. But the belts matched the dad's, clearly a vacation purchase, and they were looking good together!

Here's to the father who watched his teenager knock over an entire bottle of water and, with only a sympathetic smile, helped mop up the spill. Without complaint, he bought his son another bottle at $3.95.

Here's to yet another dad who promised his daughter that he would sit next to a stranger so that she could have the window seat.

And don't forget the grandfather who immediately handed over his earphones after his grandson had broken his own by ripping the package open with a little too much gusto.

There were other men who were not as patient, understanding, or caring. But this is not to shame them. Instead, we can highlight kindness and graciousness—little acts that actually mean so much, especially when traveling out of our element.

There was a dad who, as the flight attendant explained the protocols in the event of a disaster, wordlessly put his big hand over his teenage daughter's hand, as if to say, "It'll be alright," which is a promise that is ultimately out of our hands (no matter how big). Yet, holding hands is a way of promising that, no matter what, we are in this together. These are the moments that fly away; it's best to hold on while we can.

I was one of the grateful guys greeted by loved ones at the baggage claim and, as my children tackled me to the floor with their exuberant hugs, I'd like to thank my fellow travelers for smiling as they graciously stepped aside.

In Praise of Mischief

My two sons each have a best friend in their elementary school class. These boys are kind, funny, and respectful.

And what I also love about these best friends is that, with my sons, they get into mischief.

Let me be clear—I don't condone any behavior that puts anyone in harm's way or seeks to hurt others, including their feelings. A good rule sets a limit on behavior for everyone's safety and leads to an environment that can foster well-being.

But mischief can be seen in a positive light. Mischief makers are found in mythologies across the world from Chinese legends about the Monkey King to Indonesian folk tales of Kancil, a tiny deer. True enough, Loki was a troublemaking Norse god. But the spider Anansi was the hero of many Ghanaian stories. And while Jacob, the heel-grabber of the Old Testament, was outright devious, it's also true that there was a larger good that came out of his schemes.

In terms of "good-hearted" mischief, I have in mind actions that prompt an adult's immediate eye roll, but later make a humorous story. We chuckle, "Those two are thick as thieves!" Think of Fred and George Weasley and their schemes at Hogwarts!

A little good-hearted mischief helps to seal friendships.

I didn't have a lot of friends as a child. I was the type of kid who tried to follow all of the rules all of the time. That's a lot of pressure to put on yourself. As I grew up, this rule-following morphed into a desire to please people. To riff on the great Bob Marley, you can't please all the people all the time. There are conflicting expectations in the adult world. One of the positive roles of mischief is to poke fun at rules that exist merely for the sake of rules and help us take ourselves less seriously.

What's more, a child's process of maturation is based, in part, on self-differentiation, meaning that kids need to push boundaries to discover who they are. I am in no way advocating dangerous behaviors like alcohol or drug abuse.

But the desire to be different is not wrong—it's holy to be who you were created to be, uniquely and wonderfully you (Psalm 139:14). A dear friend can help that process of self-discovery.

As I see my childhood rule-following tendencies in both my sons, I'm grateful that each one has a buddy who helps him loosen up a little. Color outside the lines! They share their secrets with their friends, and that is healthy, good-hearted, even sacred mischief. I like to see little kids wiggling and older kids seeking wiggle room in the rules. And I suspect many wise educators would agree.

At the most recent parent-teacher conference, my younger son's teacher made it clear that our child needed more reading practice, and so she was going to separate him from his best friend at certain points in the day when schoolwork was expected. But first, she led with appreciation: "I'm so glad that those two have each other. They make us all laugh!"

Dad's Rules for Decorating Your Christmas Tree

CHRISTMAS IS THE TIME for one of my favorite family rituals. I love that people from different cultural and religious backgrounds still drag a live evergreen into their homes for a few weeks and hang all kinds of shiny things on it within reach of young children and rambunctious pets. What could go wrong?

Pour yourself an eggnog and get ready for one dad's hard-won advice on how to decorate your Christmas tree. Here we go!

1. Be sure to plug in the strands of Christmas lights to test that they all work before you string them on your tree. The worst is going through all that effort to discover a strand of lights doesn't work.

2. Don't let your new puppy nose around the open box of Christmas tree ornaments. Give her a CBD gummy for dogs and put her in the backyard.

3. Don't let your kids play *Floor Is Lava* with the most breakable ornaments. Tell them to sit and be quiet. When that doesn't work, give them chew toys.

4. Don't let your kids play dodgeball with the most breakable ornaments. Where are those gummies?

5. Have plenty of Christmas cookies on hand or your kids will chew up your furniture.

6. String the lights from the top of the tree to the bottom. Perhaps, like me, you are over six feet tall and would not require a stepladder. Except that you may also be like me and your kids convinced you to purchase a tree that makes NBA players look the size of garden gnomes.

7. Obtaining the stepladder from the deep recesses of the attic will require a complicated and dramatic rescue operation. The garden gnomes have encamped up there for the winter. Don't negotiate.

8. Once you are finally finished stringing the tree, and the kids have wrecked all the furniture, it is time to hang ornaments . . .

9. But you forgot rule #1! Now a section in the middle of the gargantuan tree is completely dark. Your spouse is in something other than the Christmas spirit.

10. More eggnog!

11. Finally, the tree is all lit up. Time for the ornaments! Young children tend to hang ornaments like they play soccer—in one big clump. If they insist that all nine *Frozen* ornaments should hang on the same branch, let it go, let it go.

12. In order to get a certain Disney soundtrack out of your head, play Christmas carols.

13. Did you know that Alexa can play 250 versions of "Jingle Bell Rock"? Your kids do.

14. Hang the most precious ornaments on top of the tree, including the one from your honeymoon. What a great time that was . . . so relaxing . . .

15. Why is the puppy sprinting laps around the backyard? What was in those gummies?

16. When the tree is fully decorated, settle back on the couch to bask in its glow with your beloved ones and the pooped pooch. Teach the kids all three of the words to "O Christmas Tree" and repeat, repeat the sounding joy.

Whatever your religious beliefs, the size of your family, or height of your tree, 'tis the season for holding loved ones close as lights shine in the dark. So, Merry Christmas, Happy Holidays, and cheers. This is really good eggnog.

In Defense of Santa Claus

IF YOU HAVE BEEN reading closely, you know that most of the parenting wisdom in this book is gleaned from my mistakes. For serious questions, however, I go to the experts.

Here is the evidence mounted by a formidable group of kindergartners at my church in defense of the existence of Santa Claus.

Exhibit A: Testimonial Evidence

They told me that three first-graders reported unidentified flying streaks across the night sky last Christmas Eve. *First-graders.*

Exhibit B: Forensic Evidence

One child reported that, last year, she discovered cookie crumbs left on the plate. Ah, you say, anyone could have eaten those cookies . . .

But these cookies were *oatmeal* cookies and everyone in her family *hates* oatmeal cookies!

Exhibit C: Further Testimony

Parents all confirm the existence of Santa. And collectively, their parents agree on nothing else.

Exhibit D: Scientific Evidence

Time is relative, as Einstein proved, and kindergartners know from experience. Just think of how long they have to wait for Christmas morning! By logical extension, time would slow down for Santa to make all his deliveries in a single evening.

Exhibit E: DNA Evidence

Santa's reindeer are born able to fly.

Exhibit F: Circumstantial Evidence

Amazon delivers packages on the front steps all year long—and they don't even have flying reindeer! While familiar with those types of deliveries, I questioned the use of circumstantial evidence, which may not bear the weight of scrutiny in a court of law or, in this case, public opinion. A child shook her head: "You ask too many questions."

Duly chastised, I left them to more immediate matters—the playground—and, as is written in the holy script of *Alice in Wonderland*, resolved to believe six impossible things before breakfast.

That evening, I reported my findings to my own first-grader. He nodded wisely, "Besides, the presents always get here on time, and I just don't think *you*, Dad, could pull it off."

The defense rests its case.

Making My Kids Go to Church on Christmas Morning

It's easy when your parent is a pastor—said no preacher's kid ever! Having grown up as a PK, I have empathy for my own children's plight. Sure, there are a few perks when you are young, such as weekday access to the toys in the nursery. Maybe someone slips you extra cookies in the fellowship hall. But the cookie crumbles; the luster of basking in the glow of extra attention fades.

Just a year ago, my son bragged to his kindergarten class, "My dad is the boss of the church!" But this year, such illusions of grandeur have burned down faster than Clark Griswold's Christmas tree. His dad is making him go to church . . . on Christmas morning! Oh, the unfairness of it! No one else has such cruel parents!

"It's all because you're the pastor," he accused me.

He's not wrong, but I'll let you in on the truth (as long as you can keep a secret). I had actually planned to let the kids stay home on Christmas with my parents. My dad has recently retired from forty years of ministry—he's earned the morning off! In addition to their excitement with their new toys, I recognize that my children would rather relax in their pajamas. They don't want to go anywhere.

My plans changed, however, during my every-other-week breakfast with my colleague and friend. He serves a local Black Baptist church. Our congregations have met regularly over the past several years, including for Sunday afternoon worship services.

He and I have also exchanged pulpits. But we've never combined services to one location on Sunday morning, the most segregated hour in America.

Until we made plans for Christmas.

Before the pandemic, his congregation would host children from a local orphanage on Christmas Day. They would have an abbreviated worship service—which, knowing their tradition, was still longer than my usual service!—and then host Christmas brunch. There would also be gifts for their guests.

This was the first year since the COVID-19 outbreak that they were resuming this tradition and he invited us to join them. My church enthusiastically agreed. I've had more than one parishioner exclaim, "This is exactly what Christmas should be about!"

My children begged to differ: "Dad, this is going to be the worst Christmas morning ever!"

I empathize with them. But from my own experience growing up in the church, some of the most meaningful experiences were the very same situations that I initially protested—early mornings at the clothing drive, picking up trash at the Habitat for Humanity worksite, Christmas caroling at the assisted living facility. I was forced to attend and I'm sure I complained, loud and long. Yet, those experiences were formative for my faith. Even if I hadn't become a pastor, the people I encountered helped to shape the person I am today.

I asked my dad if he made my younger brother and me attend church on Christmas morning. He laughed and shook his head. I know that, as a parent, you have to pick your battles. Then again, when I was growing up, there wasn't the same kind of opportunity that my kids had this year. Maybe they'll begrudge everything about it save the doughnuts in the fellowship hall.

But maybe they will remember this experience long after they forget what toys they received from Santa.

Yosemite

A YEAR AFTER THE pandemic began, Ginny and I took our first vacation with people outside our immediate family. Our friends have children the same ages as ours, and we all spent the weekend in cabins next door to each other at a camp in the North Carolina mountains. On Saturday night, we got all our kids to bed, then met outside in the fresh, pine-scented air.

There were stories and plenty of laughter. We also grew serious about the effects the pandemic has had on us. I mentioned my receding hairline, whitening beard, and aching lower back. How I would often go to bed early, but awake feeling tired. How I was tired of being tired. Our friends nodded and shared their own examples of personal exhaustion.

Eventually, our talk shifted to the topic of camping. They all had stories of previous adventures. Ginny chuckled that meeting me had put an end to her backpacking days! I grinned back at her. It's true that my idea of "camping" generally involves indoor plumbing.

She went on to share a story from a backpacking trip she took years ago to Yosemite National Park. She and her hiking buddy had camped at the base of the famous Half Dome, a majestic slab of granite towering high above the forest. The trail to the summit is about 15 miles and climbs 5,000 feet in elevation. The last 100 yards are made with the assistance of two long, metal cables bolted into the steep rock face.

Ginny and her friend didn't think they could pull themselves up those cables to the summit if they were weighed down by their packs; however, other hikers had related sightings of grizzly bears that very morning. If they left their packs behind, bears might shred their packs to get their food. Solution? Unpack all their possessions; lay everything out in an orderly row on the ground. If a bear wanted something, she could have it. Ginny was going to make it to the summit.

I've since thought about this story as a metaphor for life, even beyond the ongoing reality of the pandemic. Most of the time, I shoulder my private struggles, concealing them from the rest of the world as I trudge ahead. I've wondered if the physical changes in my body during the pandemic—the hair loss, weight gain, fatigue—are related to my emotional struggles of being isolated and anxious. Carrying these burdens is exhausting.

David Whyte claimed that the antidote to exhaustion is not necessarily rest, but wholeheartedness. To me, that means airing the truth. Giving fear over to the light. I feel that wholeheartedness is more about the journey than the destination.

Whether hiking, building a relationship, or seeking self-awareness, take one step at a time.

Be wholehearted in laying it all out.

I know that practicing such openness is hard work, even terrifying. I would have guessed that Yosemite was named after a Native American word for grandeur, perhaps relating to the massive granite slabs like Half Dome. But "yosemite" literally means "the killers" in the Sierra Miwok language and is connected to grizzly bears. This surprising translation reminds me that the dangers are real—be they deadly bears or a deadly virus—and that we are so very vulnerable as we climb our mountains and shoulder our burdens.

I need vacations that allow me the space to let go of certain things, like worries about work and the future, and I need conversation partners who can relate to my struggles. In this sense, these friends pick up on what I'm laying down. But even more, they air out their worries, too. Together, we lighten our loads.

I'm grateful for this trip with our family friends and for the marshmallows, Pokémon cards, the camp lake, and late-night confessions. In that Saturday night conversation, I felt supported and gave support. I think I speak for the group when I say there was a connection not only to one another but to something greater than ourselves. Call it God, the universe, enlightenment, whatever you like. It was a mountaintop experience.

It was also temporary. Eventually, we went to bed. The next day, we packed up and came back down the mountain. Monday morning, I shuffled into the work week, childcare, and chores. I lugged the same emotional burdens, yet I felt lighter. I shared this written reflection with one of those friends from our vacation. She joked, "Maybe a curious bear carried off some of your baggage!"

Camping Heroes

One bright fall weekend, Ginny and I camped with our three young children at Hanging Rock State Park. None of this "glamping" in a luxury tent for us. We were going to have an authentic experience for three days and two nights in the woods. Of course, we brought along air mattresses, hammocks, a gas stove, bottled and sparkling water, and all kinds of snacks. Pulling away in our minivan loaded to the gills, she gave me a half-smile: "I wonder what we forgot."

Necessity is the mother of invention, and half the fun of camping is finding ways to make do. Forget a hammer for the tent pegs? Use a rock. Propane on the stove won't work? Cook over the campfire. When the built-in air pump fails to inflate your sleeping mattress, you curse your fate, but thank the gods that the guy in the adjacent camping site has a bicycle pump.

But some things are essential—like coffee—especially after a night with three kids tossing and turning like wiggly puppies in your tent. How did I forget the java? I even remembered my favorite cheap mug with its dog paw prints and the words YOU HAD ME AT WOOF!

The Hanging Rock General Store was only a half-mile from the park entrance. When I slumped through the door just past sunup, a smiling cashier already had a fresh pot and sold me a bag of ground beans for the percolator back at the campsite. I returned like a conquering hero to my bleary-eyed bride.

Duly caffeinated, we'd planned to lead the kids on a trek up to the famous rock overlook that gives the park its name. But the kids wanted to swim! The temperatures had dropped into the 40s the previous night, but they were still foolish, I mean adamant. What real harm could it do?

We hiked to a waterfall with pools so cold that your bare feet burned. That will wake anyone up! And turn your lips blue. My older sons eventually climbed the big rocks downstream while my daughter collected leaves into a colorful pile. She called this "my fruit salad."

Hiking back, we sang "This Land is Your Land" (I'm teaching them all the verses like Woody Guthrie would want). We were almost to the minivan when I reached into my pocket for my keys and . . . felt nothing! I hustled back to the falls, muttering a decidedly different tune. When I arrived, a bright-eyed child held my keys triumphantly in the air and chirped, "Here you go!"

After that adventure, granola bars and apples were not going to cut it. We drove into the next town and the Danbury General Store, which boasted a cheeseburger daily special. The proprietors had replaced the outdoor gas pumps with picnic tables, and we enjoyed our food with a view of the blue sky and green hills. I'm not sure I've ever had a better burger, especially not for $3.99. As we finished, the cook came out with little paper bags filled with candy for the kids.

If it takes a village to raise a child, it takes the kindness of strangers to take three kids camping and leave the woods with your sanity. Camping also affords the opportunity for the spiritual practice of discomfort. Getting out of your routine, your bubble. Making spur of the moment decisions. Following your whimsy can bring unexpected challenges that, in turn, afford the opportunity for your innocent children to overhear new curse words.

But it can also create bonds between parents and children.

When we returned to our campsite, Ginny took a well-deserved nap in the tent. Our kids talked tough about not being tired, but one by one, they eventually laid down. I heated water over the fire for another cup of coffee and watched the leaves dance in the gentle breeze and dappled light. It could not have been planned any better.

All the Smells

I TOOK OUR CAR for an errand the other day. There was a smell. A little something funky . . .

By the end of a hot day, it was ripe and downright rancid!

I made an appointment with our mechanic for the very next morning. However, I had a meeting at the same time. Like many things I drop, this chore fell into the lap of my wife, and she had to hang her head out the window to stomach the drive!

She dropped the car off and, mercifully, a young mechanic drove it into the shop. When he came back, she asked him if he had any idea where the smell was coming from.

"Ma'am," he replied, "there are several smells in your car."

"Several smells" is the now a running joke between us. And why not? As serious as it is to be a parent, we need not take ourselves too seriously. We can laugh while naming the noxious fumes, of which there really are several: the dirty sock smell, the fermenting apple core smell, the wet dog smell. To be sure, the dead mouse smell was by far the worst and—thanks to that guileless young man's repair—it is no longer necessary for a driver to hang her head out of the widow like our family pet. But kids being kids, there are always going to be smells.

Love smells.

Love smells like the sweet waft from a newborn's head as well as the eye-crossing stench of a blowout diaper. As the kids have grown, the smells have changed. Smells that are gross and lovely and sometimes puzzling in new and ever-changing ways. Love smells; you can laugh!

As I write this essay, Mother's Day is approaching. To be sure, it is a difficult and painful holiday for many. I think of people who have lost mothers and children, or who have tension, even estrangement, in their families. There are also those who are heartbroken because their dream of children was not to be.

Yet, Mother's Day remains a chance to sing of the grit, grace, and humor of the one who brought us into life and continues to play a huge part in getting many of us through it. My mentor, Brian Doyle, wrote: "For a moment this day, for many moments this May, let us gape in awe at the strength of women, and look upon their sinewy courage with respect and humility."

I say, "Amen!" to that.

In case you are wondering, there is a certain cleaning chore involving a certain vehicle that I plan to do as part of my present for a certain person. And you know what else?

There's no one else in the world with whom I'd gladly share the smells. All the smells.

You

WELL, MY LOVE, WE are eight months into being the parents of our dog, and so far, we've given our fur baby exactly two baths.

Excuse me, *you* have given the dog two baths.

Both times a bath was needed because our daughter used the poor creature's back as a paint canvas. The first time our little artist struck, I was at a church meeting. The second time was this evening when I was upstairs isolating because I'd just tested positive for COVID-19. I was half-asleep in the wicker chair in the corner when—bang!—the dog barged through the door with our half-naked daughter hot on her paws, her long hair loose and flowing behind her like corn silk. They were closely followed by our middle child, ever the helper, who chirped, "Dad, she painted her back. *Again!*"

I sprang to my feet, adrenaline surging, and grabbed the dog's collar to keep her off the duvet. Just as I started toward the master bathroom, you burst onto the scene. "Not in our tub," you cried, "I got this!" Before I could even comment on the impressive brush strokes across the dog's fur, you all left in a blur of legs and paws and hair and paint.

It's now fifteen minutes or so later. Our dog is dozing under the bed. Don't worry; I already took her outside to pee. You are now bathing the children, two of whom also have paint in their hair. This is the fourth day since I woke up with a sore throat and decided to swab my nose "just to be safe." One more day and I should be able to lend more of a hand. Still, you remain resolute. You always are.

In less than a month, you will run over a hundred miles with a team of nine other women through the Blue Ridge Mountains, then return home in time to pack lunches and get the kids off to school. Probably walk the dog, too.

The world is precarious and fraught with danger.

But just earlier, I heard you instructing the kids over the running bath water as you bathed the whiny puppy: "She needs you to be calm. If you're calm, it will help."

I am listening to you.

www.ingramcontent.com/pod-product-compliance
Lightning Source LLC
Chambersburg PA
CBHW070739030726
47601CB00001B/66